McClellan's essays are unique contributions to our understanding of a distinguished literature which has only recently begun to be seriously explored in this country and will prove to be indispensable to those interested in the development of the modern Japanese novel.

EDWIN MCCLELLAN was born in Japan in 1925. He was an undergraduate at the University of Saint Andrews in Scotland and later received his Ph.D. from the University of Chicago, where he is now professor of Japanese literature and chairman of the Department of Far Eastern Languages and Civilizations. His translation of Sōseki's *Kokoro* was published in 1957 and reprinted under UNESCO sponsorship in 1967. His articles and essays have appeared in the *Harvard Journal of Asiatic Studies, The New Yorker, The Chicago Review*, and elsewhere. In conjunction with *Two Japanese Novelists* the University of Chicago Press is publishing McClellan's translation of Sōseki's *Grass on the Wayside*, an autobiographical novel rich in the reconstruction of human relationships.

Two Japanese Novelists

Two Japanese Novelists

Sōseki and Tōson

Edwin McClellan

The University of Chicago Press

Chicago and London

Library of Congress Catalog Card Number: 76-81223

THE UNIVERSITY OF CHICAGO PRESS, CHICAGO 60637
THE UNIVERSITY OF CHICAGO PRESS, LTD., LONDON W.C. 1

© *1969 by the University of Chicago*
All rights reserved. Published 1969
Printed in Great Britain

To David Grene

Contents

Preface

The Western reader who is acquainted with Lady Murasaki's *The Tale of Genji*, which has often enough been called the world's first great novel, and the works of such accomplished contemporary writers as Tanizaki Jun'ichirō, Kawabata Yasunari, and Mishima Yukio, may be a little surprised to learn that the modern Japanese novel has a very short history indeed, that it reached its maturity only in the first decade of this century, when men like Sōseki (1867–1916) and Tōson (1872–1943) began to write, and that it came into being, as did so much else in modern Japan, mostly as a result of the Western impact.

This is not to say that Sōseki and Tōson were in any important way imitative; for though they were inspired by Western models, they fully retained throughout their careers their Japanese identity, and their vision was all their own. But they inherited very little, if anything, from the native tradition, Lady Murasaki notwithstanding. And in this sense they were truly pioneers.

One of the more curious features of Japanese literary history is that *The Tale of Genji* should stand so alone, that for so many hundreds of years after Lady Murasaki's death, no writer should have appeared who shared her conception of the novel as a means of saying something profoundly true about people. Perhaps the decline soon after her death of her class, the civil aristocracy, with its insatiable curiosity about human behavior and impatience with abstractions, had something to do with it. At any rate, it would appear that by the time of the last of the military regimes, that of the Tokugawa (1600–1868), fiction had come to be regarded as a vulgar and frivolous art, lacking the discipline of Nō or the "truthfulness" of poetry. And indeed, during that era, neither those who read fiction nor those who wrote it approached it with much seriousness.

It was with some surprise, then, that the Japanese discovered after the Meiji Restoration of 1868 that such eminently respectable men as Disraeli and Bulwer-Lytton had actually won reputations for themselves as novelists, and that the content of at least some Western novels seemed to indicate a certain solemnity of purpose. But of course such discovery did not lead immediately to a change in the condition of a pursuit unrespected for so long. And for almost forty years, until the beginning of the twentieth century, Japanese fiction continued to be of rather low quality generally.

This was a period of transition in Japanese literature, when there was little assurance to be found either in the old or in the new. And it came to an end only when such men as Sōseki and Tōson, who were of the first Meiji generation, reached their maturity. Unlike their predecessors, these men had been exposed to Western ideas and books in their adolescence; they were thoroughly modern men, who had grown up in an atmosphere of destruction and progress, of doubt and self-assertion, so that when they began to write, they did so not as superficial imitators of a Western literary form but as modern Japanese who found the realistic novel the most congenial means of expressing themselves.

By this time too, the written language at the disposal of the novelist, which for many years after the Restoration had retained much of the florid, semi-classical style of Tokugawa romances, had undergone sufficient change to allow Sōseki and Tōson to shape a language which closely resembled that of everyday speech, and which was precise enough for their purpose. In other words, they were among the very first writers to use a language which would not seem particularly old-fashioned or difficult to the ordinarily well-educated Japanese today. Even here, then, they were pioneers.

Japanese critics have only too often reminded us of the great differences between Sōseki and Tōson. And certainly they are very different. Sōseki is much the more flamboyant of the two, by far the better storyteller. By Japanese standards at least, most of his novels are quite dramatic, with clearly articulated themes. His characters, whether tragic or comic, are conceived with a certain intellectual boldness and, in his later novels, with remarkable psychological insight. Tōson, by comparison, may seem rather limited. He has little of the virtuosity, or the versatility, of Sōseki. His characters, though convincingly enough drawn, tend to be shadowy figures, and seem to be the creations of a cautious mind which is fearful of imposing itself. And we find that, unlike

Sōseki, he is often at his best when he is being more of an essayist, or a prose lyricist, than a storyteller.

In their separate attempts to introduce a new kind of realism, the two brought with them different conceptions of what the novel ought to be. What Sōseki wanted to do was to combine in his novels modern intellectuality with dramatic effectiveness. He was a distinguished academic turned novelist, which fact alone made him an unprecedented phenomenon. But what was perhaps more important was his insistence that a novelist should above all be a storyteller. Here he was more Westernized than Tōson, who apparently never rid himself of certain traditional prejudices of the educated Japanese towards fiction. Tōson began his career as a lyrical poet; and in his maturity, he seemed to regard the storyteller's need to fabricate as a sort of indulgence, and to believe that his contribution to the novel should be by way of bringing to it the "truthfulness," the "sincerity," of the poet or the essayist. Thus in his entire career, he wrote only one novel—his first— around imaginary persons. All the others are concerned either with himself or with his family. Whereas only one of Sōseki's novels—his last to be completed—is more or less a record of actual happenings.

Of all the writers of their time, these two were probably the most influential.[1] Nowhere in the world has the autobiographical novel flourished as it has in Japan since Tōson's time. And perhaps much of the suspicion that still lingers there towards the imaginative storyteller is owing to his influence. On the other hand, it is equally likely that had Sōseki never lived, there would have been less audacity in Japanese fiction today.

But for all their differences, they were both very much children of Meiji. They were uprooted people, intellectually and socially; and as novelists, their major concern was to depict the condition of those who had had to pay a price for having been born in a time of

1. Many Japanese critics would no doubt consider Mori Ōgai (1862–1922) more important than Tōson. It is true that Ōgai was generally a more formidable intellectual figure than Tōson; and as stylist, critic, essayist, and translator, he probably had no equal among his contemporaries. But as novelist, he seems to have lacked originality and imagination. His historical novellas, for which he is perhaps most admired, are indeed distinguished. But for all their dignity and somber beauty, they are much too academic in tone and intention to be enjoyed as fiction. Ōgai, one feels, was basically a professor of genius who happened to write fiction and semi-fiction at a time when his kind of intellectual distinction was a rare phenomenon in the Japanese literary world. And in the specific context of the development of the modern realistic novel in twentieth-century Japan, surely his contribution cannot be compared to Tōson's.

great change. One important aspect of their modernity was that they were the first to write articulately about intelligent, sensitive men for whom the values of the past had been destroyed, and who could not identify themselves with the values of a success-minded society bent on material progress. Thus their typical heroes are isolated intellectuals who, like Sensei in Sōseki's *The Heart*, and Hanzō in Tōson's *Before the Dawn*, are destroyed by loneliness.

The need to assert oneself in a world where one felt one did not belong, and the preoccupation with one's own feelings and thoughts—perhaps these were in part responsible for the fact that Sōseki and Tōson wrote with such fresh psychological insight, with such "realism." For it would seem that in Japan at least, the modern realistic novel could come into being only when men like them were ready to depict character in terms of what was intrinsically true to the individual self, rather than what was held to be true by convention.

The two essays in this volume are slightly altered versions of essays that originally appeared in the *Harvard Journal of Asiatic Studies*. I should like to thank John L. Bishop, editor of that journal, who has made my association with it a very pleasant experience. My thanks are due also to Howard S. Hibbett of Harvard University, my friends at Keiō University, Tokyo, and my teachers at the University of Chicago, whose encouragement has meant a great deal to me.

Sōseki

Natsume Kinnosuke was born in 1867 in Tokyo. He later adopted the pen name of Sōseki, which replaced, as is the custom in Japan, his given name. He is usually referred to simply as Sōseki, though his full literary name is Natsume Sōseki. His father was a well-to-do townsman holding the hereditary administrative post of *nanushi*, or "ward chief." The *nanushi* were not of the samurai class, but they were among the more privileged of the town commoners and were regarded with some awe by their neighbors. The family fortune, however, declined rapidly after the Imperial Restoration of 1868.

His childhood was unhappy. He was born when his father was fifty-three and his mother, forty. There were already five children in the family, and the birth of another son was not welcome. Not only was the family position becoming increasingly insecure, but the Natsumes felt some disgrace in having a child at their age.[1] It is said that the boy was immediately put out to nurse with a shopkeeper's wife in a nearby village. Although soon returned to his parents, he was not kept at home for long; and in 1868 he was adopted by a childless couple named Shiobara.[2] They were not unkind to him, but difficulties arose between them which eventually led to a divorce. The young boy was forced to witness many sordid scenes in his adopted home. In his ninth year, he was once more sent back to his parents. No wonder then that Sōseki later wrote that his childhood memories had "a cold and sad shadow over them."[3] That his sense of loneliness which so marked his adult life had its beginnings in early childhood, we can guess

---

1. Komiya Toyotaka, *Natsume Sōseki*, 3 vols. (Tokyo, 1953), 1: 23.

2. There seems to be some uncertainty as to when exactly the adoption took place. However, most Japanese authorities are agreed that it was in 1868; see, for example, Akamon bungakukai, ed., *Natsume Sōseki* (Tokyo, 1944); Ara Masato, *Hyōden Natsume Sōseki* (Tokyo, 1960); Etō Jun, *Natsume Sōseki* (Tokyo, 1960); Iwagami Jun'ichi, *Sōseki nyūmon* (Tokyo, 1959); Senuma Shigeki, *Natsume Sōseki* (Tokyo, 1962).

3. Sōseki zenshū kankōkai, ed., *Sōseki zenshū*, 20 vols. (Tokyo, 1928) (hereafter referred to as *Zenshū*), 13: 399.

from the following passage, which he wrote shortly before his
death:

> I was born to my parents in their evening years. I was their youngest son. The
> story that my mother was ashamed of having a baby at her age, I hear even
> now. . . . At any rate, I was sent soon afterwards to a certain couple as their
> adopted son. . . . I was with them until the age of eight or nine, when one begins
> to understand things. There was some trouble between them, so it was arranged
> that I should be returned to my parents. . . . I did not know that I had come
> back to my own home and I kept on thinking as I did before that my parents
> were my grandparents. Unsuspectingly, I continued to call them "grandma"
> and "grandpa." They on their part, thinking perhaps that it would be strange
> to change things suddenly, said nothing when I called them this. They did not
> pet me as parents do their youngest children. . . . I remember particularly that
> my father treated me rather harshly. . . . One night, the following incident took
> place. I was sleeping alone in a room when I was awakened by someone calling
> my name in a quiet voice. Frightened, I looked at the figure crouching by my
> bedside. It was dark, so I could not tell who it was. Being a child, I lay still and
> listened to what the person had to say. Then I realized that the voice belonged
> to our maid. In the darkness, the maid whispered into my ear: "These people
> that you think are your grandfather and grandmother are really your father
> and mother. I am telling you this because recently I heard them saying that
> you must in some way have sensed that they were your parents, since you
> seemed to prefer this house to the other one. They were saying how strange it
> was. You mustn't tell anybody that I told you this. Understand?" All I said
> at the time was "All right," but in my heart, I was happy. I was happy not
> because I had been told the truth, but because the maid had been so kind to me.[4]

Not much is known of Sōseki's early schooling. The modern
school system had not yet been properly organized, and at that
time Tokyo possessed only one university and one state high
school. There were, however, a few private academies which
offered education up to the college entrance standard, and it was
apparently not very difficult for an intelligent, middle-class boy to
acquire a moderately good education in those days.

"When I was at high school," Sōseki tells us, "my specialty
was idling; I did very little work."[5] He was nevertheless suffi-
ciently interested in pursuing his studies to leave the state high
school and enter a private academy where, he believed, he would
be able to learn more English. He did not study English from
choice. He liked the Chinese classics much better, but he had to
know English if he wanted to get into college.[6] English was then

4. *Zenshū*, 13: 416–18.
5. *Zenshū*, 20: 530.
6. *Zenshū*, 20: 440–41.

almost as necessary to the college student as Japanese, for Japanese educators had not yet had time to write textbooks in their own language.

He entered the college of the university in 1884, when he was seventeen. The college curriculum at that time took five years to complete. It was while he was at college that he decided to special-ize in English. Earlier, when he was about fifteen, he had been keenly interested in literature and had said to an elder brother that he might one day become a writer. The brother had admon-ished him, saying that writing was not a profession but a mere accomplishment.[7] It would seem that he succeeded in convincing Sōseki of the frivolity of a literary career, for two or three years later we find the young man telling a college friend that he was toying with the idea of becoming an architect. The reason that Sōseki himself gives us for wanting to be an architect is strange. He knew that he was a little odd, he says, and decided he would have to choose a profession that would not only afford him a living but would allow him to remain an oddity. His friend was not so prac-tical as his brother, however, and told him that there was no glory in being an architect in such a poor country as Japan, where there would never arise the opportunity of building a great monu-ment of the order of St. Paul's. This time Sōseki was encouraged to become a writer. Even in a poor country, he was told, a man could have a distinguished literary career.[8] Once more he was convinced, and decided to concentrate on the study of English literature.

It is not clear whether he meant eventually to become a novelist or a literary scholar. Probably he himself did not know. It must have been difficult for a young Japanese of that period to know what sort of career would suit him best. In a time when a great part of the educated population of Japan was engaged in indiscriminate and aimless imitation of everything Western, it is not surprising that the young Sōseki should have been so vague about his future. Besides, Japan was then short of trained men, and it was relatively easy for a young university graduate to find a decent post, regardless of the profession he had chosen for himself.

It was during Sōseki's student days that there began to appear movements against excessive Europeanization. Nationalistic

7. *Zenshū*, 20: 507.
8. *Zenshū*, 20: 507-8.

societies and magazines were founded for the purpose of extolling purely Japanese virtues. To what extent this nationalism affected college students it is difficult to say, but it would seem that it was not popular among the more intelligent at Sōseki's college.[9] There must have been enough unintelligent ones there to form a society, however, for Sōseki tells us that he once addressed such a group, pointing out the limitations of patriotism as a basis for one's actions. "Do we go to the toilet or wash our faces for our country?"[10] he asked them. He was to retain his dislike of nationalism for the rest of his life. In 1911, he said to a gathering in a small provincial town: "People have at last stopped boasting about Mt. Fuji to foreigners. They are now busy telling everyone that Japan is a first-class power. One can only marvel at the optimism of such people."[11]

Sōseki claims that the teaching of English at the university was very dull. He obviously expected much more in the way of exciting ideas than the English lecturer, J. M. Dixon (author of such books as *Dictionary of Idiomatic English Phrases, Specially Designed for the Use of Japanese Students* and *English Letter-Writing*) could provide. Instead of being told what English literature was all about, he complains, he was forced to learn when various authors were born, when their books first appeared, and other such unimportant facts.[12] Nevertheless, there is no doubt that he had attained a surprising mastery of the English language by the time he graduated. He was able to read English with ease, and he could write it with a fluency that must have been far beyond the ability of the average student. The following is the opening passage of his translation, written in 1891, of the twelfth-century Japanese piece, *Hōjō-ki* (*Notes of a Recluse*):

> Incessant is the change of water here where the stream glides on calmly: the spray appears over a cataract, yet vanishes without a moment's delay. Walls standing side by side, tilings vying with one another in loftiness, these are from generations past the abodes of high and low in a mighty town. But none of them has resisted the destructive work of time. Some stand in ruins: others are replaced by new structures. Their possessors too share the same fate with them. Let the place be the same, the people as numerous as before, yet we can scarcely meet one out of every ten with whom we had long ago a chance of coming across. We see our first light in the morning and return to our long home

9. Komiya Toyotaka, *Shirarezaru Sōseki* (Tokyo, 1951), p. 57.
10. *Zenshū*, 14: 379.
11. *Zenshū*, 14: 280.
12. *Zenshū*, 14: 362.

next evening. Our destiny is like bubbles of water. Whence do we come? Whither do we tend? What ails us, what delights us in the unreal world? It is impossible to say.[13]

He tried his hand at writing English verse too, but here he was remarkably unsuccessful. He once confessed that he had no ear for English poetry and that the subtleties of its music eluded him.[14] This statement is all the more significant when one remembers that he was a respected writer of haiku. Here is a poem by him, probably written around the turn of the century:

> Lonely I sit in my lonesome chamber
>   And cricket chirps.
> My lamp lies lonely half in slumber
>   And cricket chirps.
>
> Soul, in dim conscious delight
>   In cricket chirps,
> Lost and forlorn, forlorn and bright
>   With cricket chirps.
>
> Is it my soul or only cricket
> That chirps so lonely in my chamber?
>   Still cricket chirps,
>   Chirping
> Chin—chi—ro—rin [15]

He graduated from the university in July, 1893. He had entered it in 1890, after completing the five-year course at the college. He had had a distinguished record and was soon appointed to a post at the Tokyo Normal College. It would seem that he was not too flattered by the appointment. Perhaps he was disappointed that the tentative offer made earlier by the college of the university had not materialized; but it is more likely that he could not visualize himself as a dedicated teacher and that no academic offer, short of a university lectureship, would have pleased him. Some years later he wrote: "It was suggested to me that I should teach. I had no desire to teach, or not to teach."[16]

Two years later, in 1895, he accepted an offer from the high school in Matsuyama; in April, he left Tokyo for the small castle town in Shikoku. There seems to be no satisfactory explanation of

13. *Zenshū*, 20: 261.
14. *Zenshū*, 20: 552.
15. *Zenshū*, 15: 243.
16. *Zenshū*, 20: 510.

why he did such an extraordinary thing. It was no trivial matter for a man born and bred in Tokyo, and a distinguished graduate of the university at that, to become a teacher in an unimportant provincial high school. Komiya Toyotaka, his friend and biographer, quotes him as saying that he had left Tokyo and gone to Matsuyama "in the spirit of renouncing everything."[17] Perhaps there was some spiritual significance in the self-inflicted exile, then, for that very year he visited a Zen temple in Kamakura.

His early novel *Little Master* (*Botchan*) is about Matsuyama and its high school. In it the hero, an innocent and not too intelligent young man from Tokyo, eventually leaves Matsuyama, disgusted with the crudeness of the students and the intrigues of his colleagues. The reader not unreasonably surmises that the novel is largely autobiographical and that the author's experiences at the school were not unlike those of his hero. Actually, Sōseki was not so unhappy there. He was apparently respected by his colleagues and became quite fond of his students.[18] And he later denied that *Little Master* was in any way autobiographical.[19]

While he was at Matsuyama, he became engaged to Nakane Kyōko, the eldest daughter of the then chief secretary of the House of Peers. The Nakane family first heard of Sōseki, Kyōko tells us in her memoirs, through a chess companion of her grandfather. Her father then became more interested in Sōseki when a young lawyer whom he met by chance on a train told him that Sōseki's reputation at the university had been good.

"Look here, do you happen to know a product of the literature department by the name of Natsume Kinnosuke? I wonder what sort of a fellow he is?"

"I don't know much about him, but he was rather well thought of at the university."

"Well, there is talk of marriage between him and my daughter."

"Oh, in that case, I'll find out more about him. I can do it quite easily."

The report was indeed very favorable. My father became quite keen, and decided there should be an exchange of photographs. I had a new photograph taken, and it was sent. Soon afterwards, a photograph arrived from the other party.

I was then nineteen years old. Being of marriageable age, there had already been offers. I do not say that I was flooded with them, but I had by then seen quite a few photographs. Of course, I had been brought up in the old-fashioned way of those days, and no doubt I would have obediently accepted an offer

17. Komiya, *Natsume Sōseki*, 1: 254.
18. *Ibid.*, p. 271.
19. *Zenshū*, 20: 479.

whether I liked the looks of the man or not, had my parents wished me to do so. But none of the photographs had impressed me so favorably as to induce me to commit myself to marriage. Besides, it would seem that my father was not too enthusiastic about any of the suitors. But this particular party, when I saw the photograph, pleased me very much. There was a gentlemanly and quietly settled air about him. His eyes were steady, and there was on his face a calm and trustworthy expression. . . . Then one day he suddenly appeared wearing a frockcoat. It was the twenty-eighth of December, 1895.[20]

Kyōko liked Sōseki despite his eccentric ways, and Sōseki took a liking to his future bride because "though she had bad teeth, she made no attempt to hide them."[21] They became officially engaged.

In the following year, Sōseki accepted an offer from the Fifth National College at Kumamoto in Kyūshū. He had enjoyed a privileged position in Matsuyama—his salary was more than that of the headmaster—but he had made no friends there. At Kumamoto he would have colleagues with an academic background similar to his own. Also, his fiancée was from a family of some social standing, and he must have felt obliged to better his position. "My father showed some insight," writes Kyōko, "in agreeing to marry his daughter to him, who was then a somewhat unfashionable high school teacher."[22]

In June of that year, Mr. Nakane escorted his daughter to Kumamoto; and there the marriage ceremony, almost comical in its haphazard arrangement, took place. One of Sōseki's first remarks to his new bride was: "I am a scholar and therefore must study. I have no time to fuss over you. Please understand this."[23] Their married life in Kumamoto, however, seems to have been happy. One suspects that his four years there were the happiest in his life. Kyōko, though hopeless as a housekeeper, was cheerful and patient; and Sōseki seems to have enjoyed having a home of his own, where he could play host to his eccentric friends and students. It was while they were at Kumamoto that their first child, a girl, was born.

In June, 1900, he was offered a scholarship by his government to go to England for two years to study the English language. He first told his superiors at the college that he did not want to

20. Natsume Kyōko, *Sōseki no omoide* (Tokyo, 1929), pp. 13–14.
21. *Ibid.*, p. 17.
22. *Ibid.*, p. 20.
23. *Ibid.*, p. 27.

leave,[24] but he was finally convinced that he should go. He really had no choice, for the offer had been more an order than an invitation. He sailed from Yokohama in September, leaving his wife and child behind, and reached England at the end of the following month.

His yearly stipend as a government scholar was eighteen hundred yen. This was by no means a small sum in Japan, but it was not enough to enable Sōseki to live as respectably in London as he would have wished. He was thirty-three and on the staff of a good Japanese college; he was not unknown in his country's academic world, for university graduates with good records behind them formed in those days a fairly tightly knit intellectual aristocracy. He had never been rich, it is true, but it did not take much money to live tastefully in Japan. It must have been a terrible experience for him, then, to have to live the life of a poor student in a strange city, in small, dark rooms in shabby boarding houses. It is not surprising that he hated his stay in England and that it remained a bitter memory for him for the rest of his life. Years later, in *Grass on the Wayside (Michikusa)*, his one autobiographical novel, he wrote:

Kenzō [i.e., Sōseki] and his Japanese acquaintance stayed in the same lodging house for a time. The man's apartment had a living room in addition to the bedroom, and in the evenings he would appear in an embroidered satin dressing gown, sit down contentedly in front of the fire and read. Kenzō, who lived like a frightened mouse in a cell-like room that faced the north, secretly envied him.

Kenzō remembered too with some sadness how he had sometimes economized on his lunch. Once he bought a sandwich on his way back to the lodging house and munched it as he wandered about aimlessly in a large park. In one hand he held his umbrella with which he tried to ward off the rain that blew toward him at a slant; in his other hand he held the slices of bread with the thinly cut meat between them. It was very difficult to eat like that, and more than once he hesitated before a bench, wondering whether he should sit down. But the benches were all soaking wet.

Sometimes he would open a tin of biscuits in his room, and chew the dry, crumbly things until they felt wet enough to go down his throat. If he had had some hot water even, it would not have been such an ordeal.

At other times he would eat meager one-course meals in questionable restaurants patronized by cabmen and laborers. They sat at a long counter, with the wall rising sheer immediately behind their backs. One could not gape about therefore, as in an ordinary restaurant. But if one wanted to, one could see at a

24. *Zenshū*, 20: 508; Komiya, *Natsume Sōseki*, 2: 54.

glance all the other customers seated in a row on either side. Their faces looked as though they had not been washed for days.[25]

Unfortunately, Sōseki went to England under the misconception that he would be free to study at any university of his choice. The remarkable thing is that the Japanese government should have sent him without explicit instructions as to how he should conduct his studies. Of course, they sent him abroad for the purpose of studying the English language rather than literature, and it may well have been their opinion that so long as Sōseki spent two years in the country, he would be able to learn the language satisfactorily. But he already had a reasonable command of spoken English, and he could hardly be expected to learn much from cockney landladies and such. He had no letters of introduction, and because he was poor, he could not—or would not—associate with members of the Japanese diplomatic or business communities in London who might have introduced him to educated Englishmen. As a result, he spent the two years in a foreign city in almost complete isolation. "The two years I spent in London were most unpleasant," he writes. "I was like a shaggy dog amongst English gentlemen."[26]

Of England and Englishmen, then, he had hardly one happy memory. Perhaps he was too proud and too ready to denounce the people whom the more superficial of his countrymen were so eager to emulate.

The first thing I had to do after landing was to decide where I should study. I was inclined to go to either Oxford or Cambridge, since they were centers of learning well-known even to us. Fortunately, I had a friend at Cambridge who invited me to visit him. And so I took the opportunity of going there to see what sort of a place it was. Besides my friend, I met two or three Japanese there. They were all sons and younger brothers of wealthy merchants, who were prepared to spend thousands of yen per year in order to become "gentlemen." My allowance from the government was 1,800 yen a year. In a place where money controlled everything, I could hardly hope to compete with these people. . . . I thought: my purpose in coming to England is different from that of these easygoing people; I do not know if the gentlemen of England are so impressive as to make it worth my while to imitate them; besides, having already spent my youth in the Orient, why should I now start learning how to conduct myself from these English gentlemen who are younger than I am?[27]

Guessing that Oxford would be no different, he did not bother to go there. He thought of going to Edinburgh or Dublin, but decided against it. Here he showed the prejudice of the Tokyo Japanese against provincial cities. He was afraid that the English spoken in those cities would not be "pure" and that he would run the risk of picking up a provincial accent.

And so he decided to stay in London. He attended a course at the university but was not impressed by it. Finally, he began taking private lessons from W. J. Craig, the editor of the *Arden Shakespeare*. It is doubtful that Sōseki learned much from him, for Craig, the typical absent-minded scholar, seemed often unaware of matters not directly concerning his work. He was an Irishman, however, and he seemed to share Sōseki's lack of enthusiasm for Englishmen. Sōseki writes: "Once, he stuck his head out of the window, and looked down at the people walking busily along the street and said to me: 'Of all those people down there, not more than one in a hundred would understand poetry. What a pitiful lot.'"[28]

His unhappiness was such that towards the end of his stay in England, he began to show definite signs of a nervous breakdown. He had spent most of his time alone in his room, reading furiously. Two years of loneliness and overwork left a permanent mark on Sōseki; and he returned to Japan an irritable man, prone to sudden outbursts of temper and more eccentric than ever. He must have behaved strangely in London, for it began to be rumored among his fellow Japanese there that he had gone mad; indeed, it would seem that one of them went to the trouble of reporting his "madness" to the Ministry of Education in Tokyo.[29] There can be no doubt, however, that his lonely stay in England benefited him greatly as a prospective novelist. It was there that he despaired of ever grasping the essence of a foreign literary tradition and decided that in the future he would have to find his *raison d'être*, not as a student of another country's literature, but as a pioneer within his own culture, whose opinions and standards, whether original or not, were at least the result of honest and independent inquiry. In those days, Sōseki tells us, Japanese believed anything so long as a Westerner had said it; but as an independent Japanese, he had to find out for himself what was good and what was bad.

28. *Zenshū*, 13: 121.
29. Komiya, *Natsume Sōseki*, 2: 112–13.

"It was the honest thing to do." In order, then, to give himself a basis for independent judgment, he started reading works on subjects far removed from literature, such as science and philosophy.[30]

He himself admits that there was a certain amount of naïveté in his decision. But perhaps a person of his quality should be judged not by the complexity of his ideas but by the depth of experience that leads him to them.

We would be wrong to assume that he returned to Japan a confirmed hater of the West. He asserted his independence not so much as a Japanese but as an individual, and this sense of his own integrity which stayed with him throughout his life, though not acquired because of his visit to England, was given greater articulation through his understanding of what personal freedom meant to Englishmen. In a lecture on individualism given some years later, in which he defined individualism not as selfishness but as a point of view which respected the freedom of others and which considered the right and wrong of a situation whatever the crowd might say, he said:

... England is a country where freedom is very sacred, as you all know. However, though she loves freedom, there is no country that respects order more. To tell the truth, I have no liking for England. But I must be honest, whether I like the country or not. I do not think there is a place in the world so free or so orderly.[31]

What one likes about Sōseki's attitude towards the West is that while he hated jingoists in his own country, he disliked just as much those Japanese who saw nothing good in things Japanese. He wrote in 1905:

It seems to be the fashion these days to imitate uncritically the works of anyone who has made a name for himself in the West. There is much that is questionable being written there. It would be a pity to lose one's own and one's country's special characteristics through too much adoration of the West. . . . Writers must imitate literary techniques simply to develop those qualities peculiar to ourselves.[32]

On the other hand, he points out, as a reaction against indiscriminate imitation, there has been also a tendency towards indiscriminate espousal of Japanese traditions. "Unfortunately, in

30. *Zenshū*, 14: 363–64.
31. *Zenshū*, 14: 373.
32. *Zenshū*, 20: 422–23.

literature, I do not think we possess anything in our past that we can proudly compare with the literature of the West."[33]

He arrived in Japan in January, 1903. He did not return to Kumamoto, but was appointed in April to the First National College in Tokyo. He was also given the lectureship in English literature that Lafcadio Hearn had held immediately before him at the Imperial University. We are told that he complained bitterly about the latter appointment, saying that it was wrong that he should succeed such an able man as Lafcadio Hearn.[34]

He did not enjoy teaching, but the condition under which he had been awarded the scholarship to England was that he would teach for four years after his return. He remained in the academic world until 1907, when he became an employee of the *Asahi Newspaper*, which offered him a monthly salary of two hundred yen with bonuses, provided he would publish his novels in serial form in that newspaper. He had by this time established his reputation as a novelist through the publication of *I am a Cat* (*Wagahai wa neko de aru*), *Little Master*, *Pillow of Grass* (*Kusamakura*), and *Autumn Wind* (*Nowaki*). From then until his death he remained a professional writer and never returned to the university.

How drastic a step this was, we can well imagine. He was being considered for a professorship at the university at about this time, and it was no small matter for a man of his age to leave a promising career at the most distinguished university in Japan to become a writer whose livelihood depended on his ability to produce at least one novel a year.[35]

That he was well aware of the risk he was taking is shown in a letter he wrote to a friend in March, 1907, the year he resigned from the university. In it he admits that he does not know how much or how well he will be able to write in the future, and that a professorship at the university would have meant great prestige and security. But, we gather from the letter, he was disgusted by the vanity displayed by his colleagues, and the glory attached to being a professor was, for him, a meaningless thing.[36] Of course we must not overlook the economic factor, for he then had four daughters, and another child, a son, was soon to be born. He had found that he could not support his family comfortably on a

33. *Zenshū*, 20: 425–26.
34. Natsume, *Sōseki no omoide*, p. 106.
35. Komiya, *Natsume Sōseki*, 2: 247.
36. *Zenshū*, 18: 446.

lecturer's salary, and the promised increase in his income must have been attractive to him, though he was the least mercenary of men.

His resignation must have caused a minor sensation in certain circles in Tokyo. Everyone he met in the street, he tells us, looked at him strangely, and some even asked him why he had done such a thing. In his retort, which he published in the newspaper that had hired him, he insists that teaching at a university is as much a "trade" as writing for a newspaper; if it were not, he demands to know, why is it that we see professors asking for raises in their salaries?[37]

Sōseki had a deep-rooted dislike of anything that smacked of officialdom, and perhaps to him the Imperial University seemed to possess too much of the character of an official institution. Some years later, in 1911, he angrily rejected the honorary doctorate that the Ministry of Education had awarded him. He apparently wished to show publicly his contempt for all such marks of official recognition. What is perhaps more important, he felt that the government had been unforgivably arrogant in granting him the degree without first asking whether he wished to be so honored.[38]

But after all, the compelling motive for his resignation from the university was his desire to write. He had already proved to himself that he could write fiction. He was a mature man of forty, with years of preparation behind him. Perhaps he was more confident of his creative powers than he openly admitted.

I am a Cat

The first chapter of *I am a Cat* appeared in January, 1905, in the literary journal *Hototogisu*. "When the first chapter of my *Cat* appeared in *Hototogisu*," writes Sōseki, "it was my intention to stop there. But I was encouraged to continue with it, and so I wrote on, until it became as long as it is."[39] It was a great success and brought him immediate fame. Strictly speaking, it is not a novel but a series of episodes, quite unequal in merit, loosely

37. *Zenshū*, 14: 403.
38. *Zenshū*, 20: 563–67.
39. *Zenshū*, 20: 509.

strung together. As a whole, therefore, it cannot be regarded as a truly serious work.

As the title suggests, the narrator is a cat, owned by a Mr. Kushami (Mr. Sneeze). The rather obvious device of having a non-human tell the story wears thin after a while; and one begins to wonder why a man of Sōseki's taste persevered with it for almost five hundred pages.

Since Kushami's cat is the narrator, all the scenes in the novel take place either in the master's house or in the immediate neighborhood. The cat observes Kushami's personal habits and makes comments about them:

> I seldom see my master. They tell me that he is a teacher by trade. As soon as he comes back from the school, he shuts himself up in his study and hardly ever comes out. The other members of the household are under the impression that he is a tremendous scholar. He is of course pleased to have them think so. But actually he is not the hard worker that he is believed to be. I have on occasion crept quietly up to the study and caught him taking a nap. While napping, he sometimes drools over his book. He has a weak stomach, and his face has a sickly lemon-yellowish tinge to it. He is a big eater nevertheless. After a huge meal he drinks some *Takajasutaze*,[40] then retires to his study and opens a book. He becomes sleepy after two or three pages. He drools over his book. This is his nightly schedule. I am only a cat, but sometimes I find myself thinking: "Well, the life of a teacher certainly seems easy. If ever I am born a human, I must try to become a teacher. Why, if all one has to do is sleep, then surely even a cat can teach." Of course, if you ask him, he'll tell you there's nothing more strenuous than being a teacher. Every time a friend drops in, he complains bitterly and loudly about the difficulties of his profession.[41]

Sometimes the cat is altogether forgotten, and we watch Mr. Kushami's dealings with his friends and unpleasant neighbors through our own eyes.

Sōseki portrays Kushami—that is, himself—as an inwardly timid man who fondly imagines that he presents a satisfactorily haughty exterior to his wife, his children, and his plebeian neighbors. None of them takes him seriously. His neighbors in particular are inclined to treat him with contempt, for they think of him as a mere schoolteacher, almost as poor as themselves. They become the allies of Kushami's chief enemy of the neighborhood, a gross, newly rich financier by the name of Kaneda (Moneyfield), who seems to them a personification of worldly power and

40. A modified product of diastase, and a popular medicine at the time.
41. *Zenshū*, I: 5–6.

success. They, with the connivance of Kaneda, make poor Kushami's daily life miserable by resorting to such childish tricks as gathering outside his house and shouting an incongruously old-fashioned insult. "Badger! Badger! You're the badger of Imadoyaki!" Indeed, well educated though Kushami is, he is unable to grasp the exact nature of the insult which, one gathers, has some sort of legendary significance understood only by the lower classes. He rushes out, nevertheless, to admonish them. He finds that they have somehow all disappeared and goes back to his house in angry frustration.

Kaneda's daughter is being courted by a young intimate of Kushami, Kangetsu. Kangetsu is at the graduate school, endlessly grinding a glass ball in an attempt to reduce it to the right degree of convexity. The task may take him ten years, but he must succeed, for without a Ph.D. he will not win the approval of Mr. Kaneda, who does not mind scholars so long as they possess the doctor's degree. Kangetsu's courtship fails, however, and at the end of the novel, we find him giving up his glass-grinding and marrying a girl from his home town.

The insensitive businessman is a type familiar to us now, but was a relatively new phenomenon in Japan at the time Sōseki wrote his novel. That Sōseki was satirizing modern Japanese society, where a coarse-grained man of recently acquired wealth such as Kaneda could attain an almost unassailable social position, is obvious. What is perhaps more interesting to us is that so early in this century, research work for the doctor's degree had its ridiculous aspects in the eyes of a Japanese satirist.

A more subtly drawn figure is Dokusen, an acquaintance of Kushami. He wears a goatee, and the cat calls him "Mr. Philosopher." He is a professional conservative, and so articulate and convincing is he in his role that we first mistake him for a sincere and dedicated man. But we eventually find out from Meitei, a pleasant and frivolous lover of the fine arts, that Dokusen is a mountebank. The revelation comes as a shock to Kushami, at whose house Dokusen has recently made a short but powerful speech in defense of the old ways:

It may well be that Western civilization is dynamic and progressive. But it is a civilization constructed by men who are destined to live their lives in frustration. In Japanese civilization, however, one does not seek comfort in change outside of oneself. Its great difference from Western civilization lies in its tenet that external things cannot be changed fundamentally. For example, we do not, as do those of the West, try to change the relationship between parents and children simply because we find that it is not entirely pleasing to us. We try to find peace of mind by accepting the fact that the relationship between parents and children cannot be changed. Similarly, we have accepted the relationship between husbands and wives, between lords and retainers, and between samurai and commoners. Why, we view nature itself in the same way. If we cannot visit a neighboring country because there are mountains, instead of trying to move them, we try to plan our lives on the assumption that they will never be moved. We try to cultivate the state of mind which says, "Though the mountains cannot be moved, I shall be satisfied." The essence of what I am saying has been grasped by the Zennist and the Confucianist.[42]

This is satire of a very high order. At any rate, Kushami is completely taken in. "The master sat and listened," the cat comments. "He did not even say that he understood or that he did not understand. When the strange guest departed, he returned to his study. He sat still, his book unopened. He seemed to be deep in thought."

But in caricature there is always a touch of cruelty, and Sōseki must have been aware of this, for the book ends on an incongruously sad note, as though the author were trying to make some sort of amends. After having spent the afternoon in cheerful and aimless conversation, Kushami's friends are ready to leave:

It is finally evening; the short autumn day is over. The fire in the brazier has gone out. Mingled with the ashes are the corpses of cigarettes, lying in great confusion. Jolly though the company has been, it must at last have had its fill of entertainment. Mr. Dokusen is the first to get up, saying: "It is late. I think I'll go." Then one by one the rest depart, saying: "Well, I think I'll be going too." The room is suddenly lonely, like a theatre after the audience has left.

The master finishes his dinner and goes into his study.... His wife sits sewing. The children are asleep, lying side by side. The maid has gone to the public bath.

Knock on the hearts of these seemingly carefree people, and you will hear a sound that is somehow sad. Mr. Dokusen, even though he appears to have grasped the essence of the universe, must sometimes tread the earth. Mr. Meitei may be cheerful, but the world he lives in is not like the world he sees in paintings. Mr. Kangetsu has stopped grinding his glass ball and has brought back a wife from his native province. This was the reasonable and proper thing for him to do, but what a bore it would be if one had always to do the reasonable and proper thing....

The master's bad stomach will kill him sooner or later. Old man Kaneda has already died from greed. Death is the fate of all things, and if one finds nothing useful to do in life, then perhaps the most intelligent thing to do is to die early.[43]

And the cat does die shortly afterwards. He drinks his master's beer in the kitchen, then steps out in a drunken stupor and drowns. His last words are: "Lord have mercy on my soul, have mercy on my soul. I am grateful, I am grateful."

Little Master

Little Master (*Botchan*) was written in 1906. It is told in the first person, and its language is the vigorous, everyday speech of Tokyo. The style has a certain crudeness which, though fully intended, limits the range of expression and prevents the novel from having much depth. Sōseki was here trying to develop a style which was free from ornateness, and in his quest for naturalness and simplicity, he chose the familiar device of making the hero, a not very intelligent though well-bred young man, tell the tale.

He is descended from a line of *hatamoto* (shogunal retainers), and possesses the ideal samurai virtues to a fault. He knows he is not intelligent, but he is not ashamed of this fact; he has no respect for money and therefore never has any; he hates wiliness so much that he cannot recognize it in others; he despises physical cowardice and is nonplussed to find that it is almost held to be a virtue by his contemporaries; and he is intensely loyal to the few friends that he has. None of these qualities is of any use to him in the modern world, and without the protection that his hereditary rank would have given him had he been born before the Restoration, he is doomed to live the rest of his life in disappointment and failure.

The novel is, therefore, in a sense an indictment of modern society. But it is doubtful that Sōseki would have admired the young man very much in the role of an arrogant *hatamoto*. For he then would have been unbearably stupid and, with his two swords, rather dangerous.

43. *Zenshū*, 1: 461–62.

He is left an orphan early in the novel. He does not seem to regret the death of his parents very much, however, for they had never loved him.

The old man never made a pet of me. Mother always took my elder brother's side. My brother had an unpleasantly pale skin and liked to imitate female impersonators. Every time the old man saw me, he would say: "This fellow will never come to any good." Mother always said: "He is so rough. What will become of him?" True, I will never amount to anything. Look at me now. No wonder they were worried about my future. All you can say in my favor is that I've never been to prison.[44]

The only person that likes him is Kiyo, an aged woman-retainer of the family. She loves him for his honesty and simplicity, and the only wish she has is that they will be able to live together in a house with an imposing outside gate. She is old-fashioned, and for reasons known only to herself, is convinced that her Botchan will eventually be a success.

With the six hundred yen that his brother gives him after their parents' death, he gets a diploma in mathematics from a private college of doubtful repute. He is offered a post at a high school in Shikoku and leaves Kiyo behind in Tokyo.

She stood on the platform and looked at me through the train window. In a small voice she said: "Perhaps we'll never see each other again. Please take good care of yourself." Her eyes were filled with tears. I didn't cry. But I almost did. The train began to move, and I waited until I thought I was safe before I stuck my head out of the window and looked back. But she was still standing there. Somehow, she looked terribly small.[45]

He finds the high school little to his liking. The boys are malicious and rude, and he finds likable only one of the masters, a rough fellow from a warlike clan. The headmaster is a skilled exponent of double-talk and maintains order in the school mostly through his ability to confuse utterly the more honest members of the staff. Our hero nicknames him "Badger." The most dangerous man on the staff, however, is the senior master, who owes his exalted position to the fact that he is a university graduate. Much to Botchan's disgust, he always wears a red shirt and is in the habit of smoking a meerschaum pipe, which he wipes constantly with a colored silk handkerchief. The last item is particularly galling to the hero, who believes, in true samurai fashion, that such effeminacy in taste is unforgivable. "Redshirt," as Botchan

44. *Zenshū*, 2: 235.
45. *Zenshū*, 2: 244.

calls him, is fond of quoting Gorki, of whom Botchan has never heard, and carries with him the latest issue of *Teikoku Bungaku*, a smart "little magazine" of those times. He has a man Friday, who teaches art. The latter is a Tokyo townsman and shocks Botchan by telling him so when they first meet. Botchan considers it a disgrace that such a spineless aesthete should have been allowed to represent the great city and fears that the barbarians of Shikoku will have been given the wrong impression of Tokyo through contact with him.

Botchan finds life in the small town very boring, and his only entertainment is his daily bath in the local hot springs and occasional visits to the few restaurants in town. The latter are not very respectable, however, and when the students see him one evening eating noodles in a particularly shabby establishment, gossip begins. The matter is alluded to, albeit very obliquely, by Redshirt in a staff meeting.

"It would be true to say that schoolmasters are members of the upper classes. It is wrong, therefore, that they should always seek enjoyment of the material sort. To do so would adversely affect their characters. They are human, nevertheless, and they must have entertainment or they would not be able to tolerate life in a small provincial place like this. They should, therefore, go fishing, read good literature, or compose poetry whether of the old or the new school. Whatever they decide to do, they must find relaxation in those things which are lofty and spiritual."[46]

Botchan is furious. He remembers overhearing Redshirt discussing in honeyed tones with his artist friend a lady by the strange, foreign-sounding name of "Madonna." He wrongly imagines that it is a name that they, in their fondness for foreign words, have given their favorite geisha. He gets up and shouts angrily at Redshirt: "Tell me, what is so spiritual about going to see Madonna?"

But wrong as he was in this particular instance, his suspicions are proved to have been right after all. When his only friend, the wild clansman, is given notice through the machinations of Redshirt, he resigns, and the two of them waylay Redshirt and his man Friday as they are leaving a brothel. They begin by arguing, but Botchan and his friend are no match for the other two in a battle of words. Their only recourse to justice is force, and they give Redshirt and the teacher of art a severe beating.

Botchan and his friend leave the provincial town the next day.
They never see each other again. The novel ends with Botchan's
return to Tokyo.

I did not bother to go to an inn when I reached Tokyo. Carrying my suitcase,
I went straight to where Kiyo was living. "Kiyo," I said as I walked in, "I've
come home." She cried and said: "Botchan, you've come home at last." I was
very happy too, and so I blurted out: "I'll never go to the provinces again.
Kiyo, you and I will have a house of our own."

Later, someone got me a job as an assistant engineer on the metropolitan
lines. My salary was twenty-five yen a month, and the rent was six yen. Kiyo
seemed satisfied, even though there was no outside gate to our house. But the
poor soul died of pneumonia last February. She called me the day before she
died and said: "Please, as a favor, bury me in your family temple. I'll be happy
there, waiting for you to come." That's why her grave is in Yōgen-ji at
Kobinata.[47]

Pillow of Grass

Pillow of Grass appeared in 1906. Though quite different from
I am a Cat or *Little Master* in style and purpose, it still belongs to
the experimental phase of Sōseki's career. He wrote no other novel
like it. It is a work devoid of passion, a conscious attempt to
express man's deep-rooted yearning for life without emotional
involvements. It is a stylistic *tour de force* and in some ways the
most beautiful work that Sōseki wrote. He called it "a novel in
the manner of a haiku" and said that his purpose in writing it was
"to leave an impression of beauty in the reader's mind."[48]
Pillow of Grass has a fleeting, magical quality about it and seems
to be expressing a mood rather than a series of connected ideas.
We see the mountain village and its people as though through
a gentle mist. We do not want to see them more clearly, for to do
so would mean a return to harsh reality, to the world of passion
and pain. In a sense the narrator, a Tokyo painter who visits the
village in the mountains, is seeking a world that is more profoundly real than the one he has just left. But because of its very
passionlessness, what he seeks is closer to the senses than to the
mind or the heart.

47. *Zenshū*, 2: 371–72.
48. *Zenshū*, 20: 457.

So in *Pillow of Grass*, that which is hidden from us in our daily lives suddenly appears to us in the form of pine trees seen through the spring rain, so fine that it is like mist, or the village handyman with his packhorse, whom we see only for a moment on the mountain path, for they are soon hidden by the curtain of rain. Most of the descriptive passages or dialogues, when considered separately, seem at first quite purposeless and sometimes even frivolous; but each of them has a place in the whole scheme of the novel, and together they do leave a cumulative impression of haunting beauty in the reader's mind.

The villagers say that the young lady of the hotel is mad. She has recently returned, the painter learns, from an unsuccessful marriage and now lives with her father, who is more of a retired gentleman than a hotel keeper. Miss Nami is a mysterious elusive creature, who is understood only by the rector of the Zen temple. There is a streak of theatricality in her, but the painter sees that it is one of her ways of showing her independence. She too desires a life without passion. She is sometimes almost brutally frank, but she is only trying to find herself through disregard for convention. In none of the scenes is her character fully revealed, however, and it would be doing Sōseki an injustice to summarize explicitly what is really the total effect of a series of delicate suggestions.

Her remoteness is in keeping with the tone of the novel, for the painter, who is the narrator, is an equally remote person and finds her interesting only because she shares this quality with him. She is gently mocking in her conversations with him, but he does not mind; in their very impersonal world, there is no meanness. Even in her one act of charity in the novel, she maintains a certain aloofness. One day the painter, while lying hidden behind some bushes on a hill overlooking the village, sees her speaking to a shabbily dressed man. They have obviously met in secret, and the painter's curiosity is aroused. He sees her giving the man her purse. They then part. She walks towards the bushes:

"Maitre! Maitre!" she called twice. "Well, well," I thought, "so she has seen me."

"What is it?" I said, as I looked at her over the bushes. My hat fell on the grass.

"What are you doing in such a place?"

"I was lying here, composing poetry."

"Don't be dishonest. You saw what happened just now, didn't you?"

"Just now? Just now? Oh, you mean that. Yes, I saw a little."

She laughed. "Why only a little? You should have tried to see more than a little."

"Well, to tell the truth, I did see quite a bit."

"Just as I thought. Come here, won't you? Come out of the bushes."

Meekly, I stepped out.

"Did you want to stay there?"

"No, I was thinking of going back to the hotel."

"Let's go back together then."

Meekly, I went back to pick up my hat and my painting equipment. I then joined Miss Nami, and began to walk with her.

"Did you get any painting done?"

"No."

"It would seem that you haven't painted at all since your arrival."

"That is so."

"Isn't it rather disappointing to have come all this way to paint and then not paint a single picture?"

"I'm not in the least disappointed."

"Really? Why not?"

"What difference does it make whether one paints or one doesn't?"

"You are joking," she said. She then laughed. "What an easygoing person you are."

"If one can't be easygoing here, what's the point of coming to a place like this?"

"One should be easygoing no matter where one goes. Otherwise, what's the point of living? For example, I am not at all ashamed of having been seen back there."

"There is no need for you to be ashamed."

"Perhaps not. The man you saw with me—what do you think he is?"

"Well now, let me see. I don't suppose he is terribly rich."

She laughed. "You are quite right. Quite a fortuneteller, aren't you? He says he is so poor that he can't remain in Japan. He came to borrow money from me."

"Is that so. Where did he come from?"

"From the castle town."

"He certainly came a long way. And where is he going from here?"

"Manchuria, apparently."

"What does he intend to do there?"

"Do? Find some money perhaps, or die perhaps—who knows?"

I raised my eyes, and glanced quickly at her face. Around her mouth, now firmly closed, I saw a trace of a smile about to disappear. I was nonplussed.

"That man is my husband."

Her remark, like a sudden flash of lightning, caught me unawares. I was really surprised. I certainly was not expecting to be told such a thing, and she, on her part, could not have intended at first to tell me so much about herself.

"Surprised, aren't you?" said the woman.

"Yes, a little."

"As a matter of fact, he is not my husband any more. We were divorced."

"I see. And then—?"

"That's all there is to tell."

"I see. That white-walled house standing on the hill with the tangerine trees —it's very impressive. It's nicely situated too. Who owns it?"

"My elder brother. Let's stop there on our way back."

"For any particular reason?"

"Yes. I want to leave something there."

"I will come with you then."

We came to the path leading up to the house. Below us was the village. A hundred yards or so up the hill, we reached the outer gate. From there we did not go to the front door but went straight into the garden. She marched on as though she owned the house. I followed without hesitation. The garden faced the south. I noticed three or four *shuro* trees. Immediately below the mud wall stretched the tangerine orchard.

The woman sat on the edge of the veranda and said, "What a lovely view. Come and have a look."

"Yes, it is nice."

It was quiet behind the sliding doors, and there was no sign of life in the house. She seemed not to care. She sat still and relaxed, looking at the tangerine trees. I was baffled. I wondered to myself, did she really have a reason for coming here?

There was nothing left for us to say, so we silently gazed at the orchard below us. The warm noonday sun shone down on the whole face of the hill. The tangerine leaves seemed to fill our eyes with their brilliance; even their undersides were shimmering in the sunlight. Then from the shed behind the house, a cock began to crow.

"Oh dear, it must be noon," she said. "I had entirely forgotten my errand."[49]

The painter's conversation with the Zen priest too has the same unreal quality. It is as though the persons are only secondary to the surrounding beauty and calm. What they say and do really do not matter, for they are ephemeral creatures who cannot affect the great eternity that envelops them. The painter and the priest sit in a room in the rectory, sipping tea. It is night. The priest looks towards the garden and says:

"Look at the shadow of that pine tree."

"It is beautiful."

"Is that all?"

"Yes."

"But it is more than beautiful. It does not mind if the wind blows."

I drink the rest of the tea and put the cup down carefully. I stand up.

"I'll accompany you to the gate," he says, and calls the young novice. "Ryōnen! Ryōnen! The guest is leaving!"

As we come out of the rectory, we hear the cooing of the pigeons.

"There is nothing so lovable as pigeons. When I clap my hands, they all come to me. Would you like to see?"

The moon is brighter than ever. The numberless flowers of the magnolia tree rise layer upon layer towards the sky. In the silence of the spring night, the priest claps his hands. The sound is carried away by the breeze. He says, "Aren't they going to come down? Surely they will."

Ryōnen looks at me and grins slightly. The priest must think that pigeons can see at night. What a carefree life, I think to myself.

We part at the gate. I look back and see the shadows, one large and one small, on the stone pavement. Slowly, as the two walk towards the rectory, the shadows fade away.[50]

The last scene takes place in the railway station of the nearest big town. The Russo-Japanese war is on, and Nami's cousin has been conscripted. They have come to see him off. The young man's possible fate on the continent arouses no emotion in the woman's heart. But as the train begins to move, the face of her husband unexpectedly appears out of a window. He looks at her with regret and sorrow. She sees him, and her eyes betray the sudden pity that she feels. For a moment at least, her passionless world is gone and there is pain. Thus the novelist leaves the world of *Pillow of Grass*, and does not return to it.

Shortly after the novel appeared, he wrote to a friend that he could never find satisfaction in writing merely haiku-like novels, for to do so would be unmanly. He would like to write, he said, as though writing were a matter of life and death.[51]

Autumn Wind

Autumn Wind appeared in 1907. It is certainly a less distinguished novel than *Pillow of Grass*. But it is far closer in spirit to the later works of Sōseki than are its three predecessors, for he has here begun to write seriously about modern Japanese who suffer.

Autumn Wind is on the whole awkwardly and didactically written, with little in it that is left to the reader's imagination; and it is fairly obvious that when writing it, Sōseki had confidence neither in himself nor in the reader. No doubt a Western writer of the period, with Sōseki's experience and gifts, would have done much better. But one has to remember that Sōseki found no

Japanese predecessor or contemporary worthy of emulation; every time he wrote a new kind of novel, he had almost to create a new language proper to the genre, something which his Western counterparts did not have to do. When he wrote *Pillow of Grass*, he seemed to know from the start how best to express himself; with *Autumn Wind*, he was not so fortunate.

There are three principal characters in *Autumn Wind*: Shirai, Takayanagi, and Nakano. The first two are poor, the last, rich. This rather obvious contrast is again a sign of Sōseki's uneasiness, and though the characters are by no means crudely drawn, they never become fully alive. But he could never write a totally bad novel, for the simple reason that he was too shrewd an observer of people and too well-disciplined to rest satisfied with superficialities; if the three men in *Autumn Wind* are uncomfortably close to being types, they are at least complicated enough to deserve some serious consideration.

Shirai, the oldest of the three, is a university-educated man who, because of his conviction that the scholar is society's most valuable asset, is found too outspoken by the authorities of one provincial high school after another. He finally gives up teaching in disgust and returns to Tokyo to find some other means of livelihood. He becomes a lowly-paid editorial writer for a magazine and continues his fight against what he believes to be the grossly materialistic outlook of his contemporaries. What makes Sōseki's portrayal of this man sympathetic is that though there is a touch of the fanatic in him, he is entirely without malice or envy; there is no self-interest in his desire for reform, and his detestation of the rich, for example, springs not from his own poverty, but from his belief that the rich and the powerful, in their smugness, have all but destroyed the spiritual aspirations of Japanese society. He is friendless—even his wife regards him as a fanatic with an incomprehensible penchant for martyrdom—but he is quite prepared to pay the price of loneliness for his principles and never allows himself even the compensation of self-pity or bitterness.

Takayanagi, a young man recently graduated from the university, is also poor and shares Shirai's hatred of the rich. But his hatred springs from envy. He is ashamed of his poverty and condemns the rich simply because he himself has no money. He indulges in self-pity and believes that if it were not for the necessity of earning his living as a hack translator of textbooks, he would write a great novel. There is decency in the young man, however, and it is manifested in his attachment to Shirai. Shirai's poverty first attracts the young man, and very soon the latter begins to see the nobility of the other. Takayanagi has been too corrupted by his own bitterness to have any principles; he finds his salvation, therefore, in his loyalty to Shirai.

In one of the best scenes in the novel, Takayanagi discovers the difference between himself and Shirai. They meet by chance outside the great walls of Baron Iwasaki's mansion and take a walk. The young man begins to tell the other of his misfortunes. Finally, Shirai says:

"Perhaps you think you are the only lonely person in the world. But I am lonely too. There is, however, dignity in being lonely."

Takayanagi failed to understand the other's meaning.

"Did you understand?" asked Mr. Shirai.

"Dignity? Why?"

"Unless you understand what I mean, it will be impossible for you to go on living alone. You believe yourself superior to others, and you are lonely because others do not recognize your superiority—isn't that so? But surely, if your qualities were of the kind that would be easily recognized, they would not be worth much. A man who is understood by geisha and rickshaw men can't amount to very much. It is only when one thinks of oneself as the equal of geisha and rickshaw men that one becomes angry and agitated when they show contempt. If one is no better than they are, one's work will be no better than something that they might write. It is because one is superior to such people that one is able to write something worthwhile. And when they are shown a thing that is good, they will despise it, naturally."

"I am not worried about geisha and rickshaw men, sir."

"What does it matter who they are? What I say holds equally true of your fellow graduates. Why, if all university graduates were alike, then surely they would all become famous or they would all be nonentities. You, I suppose, are confident that only you, among all the graduates, will have a name that will be remembered. You must then have decided that there is indeed a great difference between yourself and the others, despite the fact that they are university men too. Isn't it rather inconsistent of you, therefore, to grumble about your talents not being recognized by them, when you have already decided that you are better than they?"

"Is it because you believe all this, sir, that you work so hard? Do you want your name to be remembered?"

"It is a little different with me. What I just said applies to you only. I spoke as I did because it was my impression that you wanted to leave a great work to posterity."

"Please tell me, if you don't mind, why you work so hard. I want to know."

"I have no trust in such a thing as reputation, and so I don't care what happens to my name. It is for my own satisfaction that I work for the good of the world. I may become infamous, my name may become odious to others— why, I may even end up mad. But what can I do about it? I work like this because if I don't, I will be dissatisfied. And I say to myself, if this is the only way I can find satisfaction, then it is the only true way for me. What can a man do but follow his own way to truth? Man is a moral creature, and so the most noble thing he can do is to follow the true way as he knows it. And if a man walks along his path to truth, why, even the gods will have to step aside to let him pass. Who cares about Iwasaki's walls?" And he laughed.[52]

Nakano, on the other hand, is rich. He is also more generous and pleasanter than his friend Takayanagi. But despite his pleasantness, he is a limited human being, for he does not know what suffering is. Early in the novel, he comes across Takayanagi sitting dejectedly on a park bench. He takes him to a restaurant and treats him to a European lunch. Takayanagi says:

"You are a fortunate fellow. You have nothing to be dejected about." He had pushed away his plate with the half-finished steak on it. He was now smoking a cigarette. He looked at his friend. His friend was busily eating. He made a quick, negative gesture with his right hand, expressing his disagreement.

"So, I have nothing to be dejected about. And having no cause for dejection, I am a sort of fatuous fellow, is that it?" he said.

Takayanagi's lips moved slightly, as though he was about to say something. But he remained silent. The other continued. "I also was at the university for three years, remember? You know very well that I have read not a few philosophical and literary works. Whatever your impression of me may be, I think I am aware of the misery that exists in the world."

"Yes, you've read about it," said Takayanagi in the manner of a man looking down at the valley from the mountain top."[53]

Nakano then insists that he too has much to worry about. But Takayanagi remains skeptical, for he knows that Nakano is a happy man who, for the sake of his friend, is trying unsuccessfully to disguise his happiness.

That Nakano cannot really sympathize with Takayanagi becomes clear when he discusses him with his pretty fiancée. This scene, incidentally, is full of passages the like of which one does not find in his later novels. The author inserts his own comments whenever he can, in a self-conscious and rather old-fashioned attempt at adding to the romantic mood of the scene; for example:

Love is earnest. It is also deep, because it is earnest. But love is also a game.

52. *Zenshū*, 3: 367–69.
53. *Zenshū*, 3: 267–68.

Being a game, it floats. The only things that lie deep and yet float are the weeds at the bottom of the sea and youthful love.[54]

But the dialogue, as nearly always, is good, and it brings out rather well the essential selfishness of two rich and happy people in love.

These spoiled yet good people play at their profound game in the beautifully decorated room. Outside the room, the cold autumn sky stretches over the world. Under it suffer Mr. Shirai and others like him. Under it the Takayanagis live their lonely lives. But these two young people are good people.

"You were with Mr. Takayanagi at the concert the other day, weren't you?" says the girl.

"Yes. I didn't mean to go with him, but I bumped into him on my way to the concert, so I asked him to join me. He was standing sadly outside the zoo, looking at the leaves that had fallen from the cherry trees. I felt rather sorry for him."

"It was good of you to ask him. Is he ill?"

"I did notice that he coughed. I shouldn't think that it's anything serious."

"But he looks pale."

"The fellow is so neurotic, he drives himself ill. When I try to comfort him, he becomes sarcastic. He's become very odd of late."

"That's too bad. What is the matter with him?"

"Who can tell? He chooses to be alone, and regards the whole world as his enemy. There is nothing I can do."

"Perhaps it's disappointment in love."

"No one has told me if it is. Perhaps we ought to find him a wife. That might do him good."

"Well, why don't you?"

"That's easier said than done. His wife would have a rather hard time with him, he's so difficult."

"But if he gets married, he may improve."

"Perhaps, but it's in his nature to be pessimistic. His illness is chronic melancholia, I think."

She laughed. "How did he get this illness?"

"I don't know. Perhaps he inherited it. Or perhaps something happened when he was a child."[55]

Takayanagi, as a matter of fact, is truly ill and eventually discovers that he is suffering from an advanced case of tuberculosis. The doctor advises him to leave Tokyo and go to a warmer place. Nakano forces him to accept a hundred yen. Takayanagi takes the money only on the condition that Nakano will accept the manuscript of the novel that he will write while he is away. It is a theatrical gesture on Takayanagi's part, but he must retain his pride.

54. *Zenshū*, 3 : 349.
55. *Zenshū*, 3 : 350–51.

He visits Shirai to tell him that he is leaving Tokyo. As he enters the living room, he finds that there is another visitor. He is a moneylender. When Takayanagi discovers that Shirai cannot pay back the loan, he suddenly produces the money that Nakano has given him and gives it to the moneylender. Shirai has a manuscript by his side, a work that no publisher will take. Takayanagi begs to be given it. The novel ends as he leaves the house with Shirai's manuscript under his arm. He will give it to Nakano.

The last scene, therefore, is rather melodramatic, and one cannot help feeling that what Sōseki was trying to suggest here deserved more careful treatment.

Takayanagi's quixotic act has a great deal of significance for him, for it is his way of admitting that the great novel he was going to write has never been more than a wishful dream. He has come to realize his own emptiness and cannot bear to live any longer in his terrible isolation. He, therefore, tries to redeem himself by sacrificing not only his selfish ambition, but also his slender hope of prolonging his life.

Sanshirō

Sanshirō, which appeared in 1908, is regarded as the first part of a trilogy, the other two parts being *And Then—* (*Sorekara*) and *The Gate* (*Mon*). It is a much more polished work than *Autumn Wind*, and belongs without question to the latter phase of Sōseki's writing career. The didactic tone of the earlier work is gone, and there is no suggestion of the stereotype in any of the main characters. It is, however, an extremely dull work. It has almost no plot and is exasperatingly uneventful. In all his later novels, except in *And Then—*, the reactions of the characters to situations are a little too passive, and even when they react violently, they seem to know that they are doing so in vain. The shadow of doom hangs over all of them, and there is nothing they can do in this life to escape it. It is only the acuteness of their suffering that gives them significance. The one heroic quality that Sōseki's heroes possess is their capacity for suffering, and his novels interest us only so long as this capacity has magnitude.

Sanshirō, the main character of the novel, is too young to move us, however. He is still too full of hope to know that pain is not momentary but a permanent condition of man's life. *Sanshirō* is really little more than an introduction to the novels that will follow, as the disillusionment of Sanshirō's first love is no more than the first step towards greater suffering. Sanshirō never appears again in Sōseki's works, but we know that he is the kind of youth for whom life holds nothing but profound disappointment. Viewed therefore as the story of a youth whose future would be like that of the more mature heroes of the later novels, *Sanshirō* has some purpose. But by itself, it seems to be without much significance.

The novel begins with Sanshirō on a train en route to Tokyo. He has just graduated from a provincial college and is going to the great city to study at the university. He is an awkward, shy youth, who has no inkling of what life in Tokyo will be like.

On the train he enters into conversation with a man much older than himself. Despite the man's indifferent manner, Sanshirō is attracted to him. The relationship deepens when they meet again by chance in Tokyo. The older man's name is Hirota, and he teaches at a college in Tokyo. Though their friendship is not the central theme of the novel, the reader guesses that it is Hirota that Sanshirō will eventually turn to for solace.

In *The Heart* (*Kokoro*), a similar friendship is treated in greater detail. It has been said that there is a suggestion of homosexuality here. Perhaps there is, but the question seems rather irrelevant. What is relevant to our understanding of the relationship is that the love of Sensei for the nameless young man in *The Heart*, and of Hirota for Sanshirō, springs from a kind of pity, while that of the younger men springs from a vague recognition of their own ultimate fate. Sensei and Hirota are irresistibly drawn to their youthful companions because they see in the latter the sensitivity to pain that they themselves have been cursed with. The older man and the younger man of course share the same characteristic of extreme loneliness; they recognize in each other a certain alienation from the world around them and come together instinctively, seeking protection and understanding.

Through a family acquaintance Sanshirō meets Mineko, whose sophistication and beauty awe him. She is a passionate girl, who is in search of a man who will lead her out of her emotional confusion, but he is too awkward to be the masterful lover that she needs. In the end Mineko marries a suave gentleman some years older than herself. Sanshirō's friend, Yojirō, who is shrewder than he is, tells him that he has been a fool to think that Mineko would marry a man her own age.

"Why? I'll tell you. Compare young men and women in their early twenties. Women, you will find, are far superior. They will always make fools of men who are no older than themselves. Even a woman doesn't want to marry someone she doesn't respect. Of course, conceited women are an exception to this rule. As for them, they can only marry men they despise or remain single. You agree, don't you, that daughters of rich men and so on are often that way. Many of them do marry and live despising their husbands. Miss Mineko is much nicer than that. Anyone who wants to court her has to be aware of the fact that she won't even think of marrying a man she doesn't admire. That's why the likes of you and me have no right to hope to marry her." [56]

Shortly before this conversation, Sanshirō goes to see Hirota. He knows by this time that he has lost Mineko. They begin to talk about marriage. Hirota is a bachelor and remarks that many men for various reasons find it difficult to marry. Sanshirō asks:

"What kind of men?"

"Well, for example—," he began to say, then became silent. He continued to puff at his cigarette. "Here's a man, a certain fellow I know. His father died early, and he grew up relying entirely on his mother. Then she became ill. Just before she died, she called him to her bedside and told him to go to Mr. X for help after her death. The boy had never heard of this man. He asked her why he should go to him rather than someone else. She said nothing. He asked again. Finally, in a faint voice she said that Mr. X was his real father.—It's only a story, of course, but let's assume that such a man exists. Wouldn't you say that he would quite naturally have little faith in marriage?"

"I doubt that there are many such men."

"No, there aren't many, but they do exist."

"But sir, you are not one of them?"

He laughed. "You have a mother, I believe."

"Yes, sir."

"And your father?"

"He is dead."

"My own mother died the year after the promulgation of the constitution." [57]

This is the only passage in the novel that gives us a hint of the tragedy of Hirota's life. It is very moving, and neither Sōseki—nor any modern Japanese writer before him—had ever written

56. *Zenshū*, 5: 290–91.
57. *Zenshū*, 5: 278–79.

dialogue so dependent for its effect on implication. One cannot but feel that he would have written a more interesting novel had he made Hirota, not Sanshirō, the principal character, for this short dialogue gives Hirota a depth which Sanshirō, because of his innocence, does not possess. And just as Sanshirō is only potentially a tragic figure, so is Sōseki at this point only potentially a tragic writer.

The young man's craving for companionship in the big city, the strangely nostalgic quality of his first love, the girl's kindness and her inevitable cruelty, her helplessness and pride, the sympathy that Hirota immediately feels for the quiet young man—all these are delicately described; but for all its polish, *Sanshirō* fails to move us.

And Then—

A year later, *And Then—* appeared. Its hero, Daisuke, is a more mature and complicated figure than Sanshirō. The novel is therefore intrinsically more interesting than its predecessor. Its one fault is that its brooding, introspective quality is maintained throughout without relief. Nevertheless, Sōseki does manage to hold the reader's interest by the sheer power of his disciplined mind. Here, more than in any of his previous works, we see what a remarkably intelligent writer Sōseki was. And if sometimes there seems to be too much of the professor left in Sōseki the novelist, the fact is that he was the first man to introduce an unashamedly reflective, or intellectual, quality to what had been traditionally regarded as a form of popular entertainment.

Daisuke without question is meant to symbolize the disillusionment of intelligent young Japanese who have reached their maturity after the Russo-Japanese War. Japan has now attained her goal of world recognition as a modern power, and the struggle for recognition has now been replaced by the struggle for survival. Industrial expansion resulting from the war has introduced a new kind of insecurity, and thus selfishness and cruelty, into Japanese society. The ethical tenets of the society, however, have not changed to meet the new needs of the people. Men, therefore, can live contentedly in this state of sharp inconsistency only if they are stupid or hypocritical. Sōseki's point is that it is the intelligent and honest men that suffer most in this kind of society.

There is nothing that Daisuke can do to prevent the increasing alienation of himself from his father, a successful financier of samurai stock who was born some years before the Restoration. Nor can he prevent the final quarrel between himself and his elder brother who, though a tolerant and not unintelligent man, cannot understand Daisuke's need to do the unconventional thing.

Daisuke is now thirty and lives alone in a house with an elderly maid and a young man-servant. He lives in idleness, on a monthly allowance that his father grudgingly gives him. Daisuke is well aware of his own unreasonableness in insisting on his independence and at the same time relying on his father for support. It is proof of Sōseki's honesty that the courageous streak in Daisuke remains hidden until near the end of the novel. Through most of the novel, he is an almost despicable figure.

The lonely and idle life that Daisuke leads inevitably makes him self-centered. More through boredom than anything else, Daisuke has become a hypochondriac, despite the fact that he has an unusually robust physique of which he is childishly proud. His slight neuroticism does not prevent him from being a very self-contained man, however, and he does not allow the discomforts of others to upset his general equanimity. The novel opens with Daisuke waking from a night's sleep:

> He looked by his pillow and saw lying on the floor a double camellia. He remembered distinctly the sound of this flower falling during the night. To his ear it had sounded like a rubber ball that had been thrown down from the ceiling above him. He had assured himself then that the sound was exaggerated by the quiet of the night. Nevertheless, he had put his right hand over his heart and felt the steady, encouraging pulse before going to sleep.[58]

The morning paper has been placed by his bedside. He glances through it and then gets up and goes to the bathroom:

> There he carefully brushed his teeth. They were strong and even, and they were a constant source of pleasure to him. He stripped to the waist and wiped his chest and shoulders in a massaging motion. His fine-textured skin seemed to glow, as though he had rubbed oil into it and then wiped it off. . . . He then combed his black hair, which did not need the help of oil to be neat. His moustache too lay neatly and obediently, covering his upper lip in tasteful

fashion. He continued to stare into the mirror as he stroked his plump cheeks. He moved his hands as a woman would when making up her face.[59]

He staves off ennui gossiping with his man-servant or, when he visits his father's house, with his sister-in-law. He visits the theatre as often as possible and occasionally goes to a geisha house. He pretends to himself that his way of life is the only possible one for a civilized man.

Outwardly at least, he is a frivolous man, and even he himself does not realize that this life without commitment cannot last forever. His irresponsibility is largely an expression of rebellion against his upbringing. His father has unwittingly alienated his son by being the strict Confucian parent with ideals impossibly out of keeping with the modern world and with his own private practices. Whether outdated or not, the old man's code of ethics has stood him in good stead, however, and he has never had reason to doubt its utility and therefore its validity. He fails to understand his younger son, whose shrewdness he has always underestimated. Whenever Daisuke visits the family house, his father lectures to him. He says on one occasion:

"A man shouldn't always think of himself. There is society to think of, and there is one's country. One cannot be fully satisfied unless one tries to do something for other people. Surely, even you can find no satisfaction in living as idly as you do. It's different with the lower classes, of course. But how can a man of your background and education be content to live in idleness? One enjoys the benefit of whatever one has learnt only when one puts it into practice. . . . You don't have to go into business if you don't like it. There is no reason to suppose that the only way to be of service to Japan is to make money. . . . I will continue to support you. After all, I may die quite soon, and I won't be able to take any of my money with me. So don't worry about your monthly allowance. But bestir yourself and do something. Do whatever you wish to do for the good of your country. You are already thirty, aren't you?"[60]

That the old man's notion of patriotism strangely coincides with his self-interest is a thought that has often occurred to Daisuke. But he sits and listens obediently, for he dares not openly oppose his father, without whose financial assistance he cannot live as comfortably as he likes. He does not dislike his father but he feels little sympathy for him.

Daisuke thought of those men of the past who felt, wept, and became excited for selfish reasons and yet managed, through their ignorance, to convince themselves that they were being completely altruistic and who, because of this conviction, were able to bend others to their will. He envied them.[61]

That Daisuke also deludes himself, we see in his conversation with Hiraoka. The latter is an old university friend who has recently returned with his wife Michiyo from a provincial city. His firm has fired him—the reader gathers that he was caught embezzling the office funds—and he is now without work. He is bitter and desperately afraid of poverty. They meet in Tokyo for the first time in three years, and each sees that the other has changed. Daisuke's personality has become more aloof and cold and Hiraoka's more twisted. Hiraoka cannot hide his envy of Daisuke's security, and his envy soon turns to ill-concealed anger when he senses Daisuke's contempt for those who struggle so hard to survive. Daisuke becomes defensive and tries to justify his kind of life. He is a little too glib perhaps, but he is not being totally insincere:

"You ask me why I don't work. That I don't is not my fault. It is really the fault of the world around us. . . . Look at Japan. She is the kind of country that can't survive unless she borrows money from the West. In spite of this, she tries to play the role of a first-class power; she tries to force her way into the company of first-class powers. . . . She is like a frog trying to be as big as a cow. Of course, she will soon burst. This struggle affects you and me, and everybody else. Because of the pressure of competition with the West, the Japanese have no time to relax and think and do something worthwhile. They are brought up in an atmosphere of tension and frugality and then are made to engage in furious activity. No wonder they are all neurotics. Talk to them, you will find they are all fools. They think of nothing except themselves and their immediate needs. Look all over Japan, and you won't find one square inch that is bright with hope. It is dark everywhere. Standing in the middle of this darkness, what can I, alone, say or do that will be of use?"[62]

Daisuke knows that he and Hiraoka will never return to their old friendship, but he does not feel much sorrow.

He knew that he and Hiraoka had finally become separated. Every time he met him, he felt as if he were speaking to him from a great distance. But in truth he felt this way about everybody he met. He thought, "Present-day society is no more than an aggregate of isolated human beings. The ground under us may be continuous, but the houses we build on it are separated. And the people who live in them have become separated from one another. What is civilization but something that makes of men isolated, helpless creatures?"[63]

61. *Zenshū,* 6: 198.
62. *Zenshū,* 6: 82–83.
63. *Zenshū,* 6: 112.

It is Michiyo who destroys Daisuke's protective coating of aloofness. He had loved her before her marriage to Hiraoka but, in his foolish desire to play the dutiful friend, had acted as mediator between Hiraoka and Michiyo. Michiyo, whose mother and brother had shortly before died of typhoid, was in no position to reject Hiraoka's suit. Though she was in love with Daisuke, she was forced to marry Hiraoka.

When Daisuke meets her again in Tokyo, he discovers that he still loves her. His love is now fortified by pity for her and regret for his past stupidity. The strain of her unhappy marriage and the recent death of her only child have undermined her health and brought her to the verge of a nervous breakdown. She behaves with great restraint towards Daisuke, but he sees that she is also in love with him and that she has never loved her husband. He realizes what a terrible thing it was that he did to her. Like Takayanagi in *Autumn Wind*, he finally admits to himself that his life thus far has been purposeless and cowardly. One day, when Michiyo visits him, he confesses his love to her with touching simplicity: "You are very necessary to me."

There is nothing they can do but tell Hiraoka the truth about themselves. There will be a scandal, followed by ostracism. But Daisuke knows that any kind of life with Michiyo will be better than a continuation of his previous loveless existence. Because of his earlier frivolity and cynicism, his courageous decision moves us all the more.

> He saw what the future held for him and prepared himself for the coming struggle. First, there would be his father to contend with, then his elder brother and his sister-in-law, and after them Hiraoka. When his battles with them were over, there would still be that great machine-like thing called society, which took absolutely no notice of a person's freedom or his sentiments. To him, society now seemed a dark monstrous thing. "I will fight them all," he thought.[64]

He writes a letter to Hiraoka, asking him to come to his house. A few days later, Hiraoka appears, and explains that he could not come sooner because he has been nursing Michiyo. There is a touch of irony here, for it is the first time in the book that Hiraoka shows he has not entirely lost his affection for Michiyo. Furthermore, Michiyo's sudden illness reminds us that Daisuke is

---

64. *Zenshū*, 6: 228.

helpless even after his acceptance of responsibility, for it is Hiraoka, not he, who can take care of her.

Daisuke asks Hiraoka to give Michiyo her freedom. After Hiraoka's initial anger has abated, Daisuke says quietly:

"You have never loved Michiyo."

"So?"

"Yes, I know, it's not my place to say so, but I must. What really matters now is that you don't love her."

"And you are blameless?"

"I love Michiyo."

"What right have you to love another man's wife?"

"It's too late now to say that. By law, you own her. But she is a human being; you can't possess her as you would a piece of furniture. You can't hope to own her heart. You can't tell her whom to love and when to love. A husband's right doesn't stretch that far. It was your duty as a husband to see to it that she loved no one else."

"All right," said Hiraoka; he seemed to be trying desperately to control his emotion: "let's say that you are right in assuming that I have never loved Michiyo." His fists were clenched. Daisuke waited for him to finish. Hiraoka then said unexpectedly: "Do you remember what happened three years ago?"

"It was three years ago that you married Michiyo."

"Yes. Do you remember everything well?"

Daisuke's mind was suddenly filled with memories. They seemed to burn like a torch in the night.

"It was you that offered to act as mediator between me and Michiyo."

"Only after you had confessed to me your desire to marry her."

"I haven't forgotten. I am still grateful to you for your goodwill then." For a moment Hiraoka seemed to be lost in thought. Then he said: "You and I had walked through Ueno and were walking down towards Yanaka. It had been raining and the road was muddy. We talked all the way from the museum, and just as we reached that bridge, you wept for me."

Daisuke was silent.

"Never have I felt so grateful for anyone's friendship as I did then. I was so happy that night, I couldn't go to sleep. The moon was out, I remember. I stayed awake until it had disappeared."

As though in a dream Daisuke said, "I was pleased too."

Hiraoka would not let Daisuke say any more. He cried out, "Why did you weep like that for me? Why did you promise to act as mediator? If you were going to do a thing like this, why didn't you ignore me that night? What did I ever do to you, that you should do such a terrible thing to me?"[65]

Characteristically, Daisuke apologizes, not for trying to take Michiyo away from Hiraoka, but for having been so stupid as to allow his sentimental and artificial notion of friendship to

65. *Zenshū,* 6: 260–62.

override his love for her. Hiraoka finally admits defeat. He agrees to let Michiyo come to Daisuke, but only after she has recovered from her present illness. Until then, he cannot permit Daisuke to see her.

Daisuke jumped up from his seat as though he had felt a sudden electric shock. "Now I know! You intend to let me see her after she is dead! That's a terrible, cruel thing to do!" He went around the table, and grabbing Hiraoka's shoulder with his right hand, began to shake him. "Terrible! Terrible!" Hiraoka saw the look of crazed fear in Daisuke's eyes. He stood up with Daisuke's hand still on his shoulder. "You know that I would never do such a thing," he said, placing his hand on Daisuke's. They looked at each other, as though the devil had possessed them both. "You must calm down."

"I am calm," Daisuke said, but his words were uttered in short, panting breaths.[66]

We too are not very sure that Hiraoka means what he says.

Soon after, Daisuke's father receives a letter from Hiraoka officially informing him of Daisuke's request to be given Michiyo. Whether Hiraoka has written the letter as an act of vengeance or merely as a necessary formality, Sōseki does not tell us. The father is furious, for he has been trying to induce his son to marry the daughter of an important provincial landowner. He has convinced himself that he wants the marriage to take place because the girl is a distant connection of a past benefactor of his. He now sends his first son to Daisuke to find out if all that Hiraoka says is true.

Pointing to Hiraoka's letter which was now lying on the table, Daisuke's elder brother asked in a low voice: "Is it all true?"

"Yes, it is," Daisuke answered simply.

The fan in his brother's hand suddenly became still. He looked shocked. For a while, the two brothers were silent. Then the elder brother said incredulously: "Whatever made you do such a stupid thing?" Daisuke remained silent. "You could have married any girl you wanted." Daisuke still refused to speak. The brother persisted: "After all, you are not an innocent child. You've been around. What was the point of spending all that money in that worldly way of yours, if you were going to end up doing such a gauche thing?"

Daisuke lacked the strength and the will to begin explaining himself at this stage. For until very recently he had thought exactly as his brother did.

"Your sister-in-law has been crying over you."

"Is that so?" said Daisuke. His words might have been uttered in a dream.

"Father is furious."

There was no response from Daisuke. He gazed at his brother as though from a distance.

66. *Zenshū*, 6: 265.

"I have always found it difficult to understand you. But I did not let that bother me, thinking that some day you would make sense to me. Now I know I've been mistaken. I have no choice but to admit that you are totally incomprehensible to me. There is nothing so dangerous in this world as incomprehensible people. One can never be sure what they will do or what they are thinking. Of course, you aren't bothered, since you can tell yourself that what you think and what you do is your own business. But what about your father's and my social position? Surely, even you must be aware of this thing called family honor?"

But these words fell on deaf ears. . . . In his heart Daisuke was confident that he had done the right thing. He was satisfied. The only person that would understand his satisfaction was Michiyo.[67]

His brother then tells him that since he has shown no inclination to apologize or to regret his foolishness, there is nothing he can do to check their father's anger. Daisuke will be disowned.

"I understand," answered Daisuke simply.

"You're a fool," said his brother in a loud voice. Daisuke did not raise his bowed head.

"You're an idiot," said his brother. "Such a glib, talkative fellow you used to be. Now, at a time like this, you behave like a deaf mute. You don't seem to care what happens to your father's name. What was the good of all that education you received?"

He picked up the letter from the table. The room was quiet except for the sound of the letter being folded. He put it back in the envelope and placed it in his pocket.

This time he spoke in a normal tone of voice: "I am going now." Daisuke bowed in polite farewell.

"I also will not see you again," said his brother as he left for the front hall.[68]

Daisuke remains in the room for a brief while after his brother's departure, then suddenly gets up and leaves the house, telling his servant that he is going to look for a job. It is oppressively hot outside, and he begins to feel that the whole world around him is burning. He jumps onto a streetcar. He gazes through the window at the street, and his eyes seem to see nothing but the color of brilliant red. He resolves to remain on the car until the hot, burning sensation in his head has dissipated.

Thus the novel ends. We do not know what will become of Daisuke and Michiyo. Indeed, we do not even know that he will see her again. Nor are we sure that the world will ever stop burning for Daisuke.

67. *Zenshū*, 6: 270–71.
68. *Zenshū*, 6: 272.

The Gate

The Gate (*Mon*) is the last of the trilogy and was written less than
a year after *And Then*—. It is a very sad novel, full of gentle compassion. Sōsuke, the main character, is a far humbler and therefore
more sympathetic figure than Daisuke. He is older and less rebel-
lious. He has ceased to struggle against the injustice of others and
the unkindness of fate. He will never be able to attain peace in this
world, however, for he is imprisoned by the memory of the
wrong he has done and by his love and pity for his wife.

It was while he was a student at the university in Kyoto that he
betrayed Yasui, a close friend. What Oyone was to Yasui,
Sōseki does not say. But we guess that she was his wife. By taking
her away from Yasui, Sōsuke not only ruined his own career, but
his friend's also. They both had to leave the university before
completing their studies—Sōsuke because he was asked to go by
the university, and Yasui because he could not bear to remain in
Kyoto any longer.

After years of wandering in the provinces, Sōsuke and Oyone
have returned to Tokyo, their native city. They are now in their
early thirties. They are childless and live quietly in a dingy house.
Sōsuke has a lowly position in the civil service which pays him
just enough to enable them to live in genteel poverty. Their life
is uneventful. They do not hope or wish to live differently, for
they have come to realize that the little happiness that remains to
them is all in each other's company. Sometimes they wonder
what has become of Yasui, who, they have heard, has gone to
Manchuria; but they do not mention his name, for each knows
that to do so would bring pain to the other.

They are dull people. In their effort to protect themselves from
the world around them, they have become insensitive to everything except to each other's suffering.

They had not always been uninterested in the lives of others in this world.
Their indifference was forced on them by society, which had pushed them into
a small corner, and then had coldly turned its back on them. . . . And finding
that they had lost breadth in their lives, they tried to find consolation in
depth.[69]

Their lives are therefore extremely monotonous. Sōsuke goes to

69. *Zenshū*, 6: 407.

work in the morning and returns in the evening. Oyone sits in the house all day, waiting for him to come back. Their dinner conversation is desultory; there is little they can talk about since they have no friends and few interests. They are hardly a fitting subject for a novel; but *The Gate* is, to my mind, the warmest of all Sōseki's novels. This may be true because, of all his heroes, Sōsuke is the most appealing. *The Heart* may on the whole be a more moving work, but there is an unpleasant streak of selfishness and coldness in Sensei, which sometimes repels us and which is not present in Sōsuke. Sensei protests that he loves his wife, but Sōseki puts no life into Sensei's love nor into his wife. Oyone has far greater reality and depth than the wife in *The Heart*, and the love between her and Sōsuke, for all its quietness, brings her, and her husband, far closer to the reader's heart. The coldness in Sensei has been brought about by K's violent death. His betrayal is far more cruel than Sōsuke's, not in intention certainly, but in its ultimate effect. As a result Sensei's humanity is at least in part destroyed by his consciousness of the enormity of his crime. Sōsuke suffers from guilt too, but his suffering has in a sense made up for his betrayal of Yasui. The mere fact that Yasui is still alive permits Sōsuke's love for Oyone to remain intact and prevents his loneliness from destroying him.

They can never be entirely forgetful of the past, and because of this, Sōsuke sometimes unwittingly loses his gentleness towards Oyone.

They lived huddled together like those upon whom the sun has never shone and who have learned to feel warmth only in each other's arms. Sometimes when their suffering became almost unbearable, Oyone would say: "But there's nothing we can do about it." And Sōsuke would say: "We'll try to bear it."

The meaning of resignation and patience, they understood; but they seemed hardly ever to feel that emotion which we call hope. They rarely spoke of the past. Indeed, they seemed to have tacitly agreed never to talk about it. Oyone would sometimes say consolingly to her husband: "I'm sure something nice will happen to us eventually. I'm sure life isn't meant to be always unhappy." Sōsuke would then feel that fate had borrowed his wife's voice and was mocking him. He would remain silent and smile bitterly. If his wife happened to say more, unaware of her husband's smile, he would say sharply: "What right have we to hope?" Oyone would then realize the effect that her words had had on her husband and become silent. They would gaze at each other and find that they had once more returned to that dark cave of their past which they themselves had dug.[70]

70. *Zenshū*, 6: 306–7.

It is not self-pity but pity for each other that gives meaning to their lives, though it adds to their suffering. One day, Sōsuke returns from a visit to their landlord and tells Oyone of the cheerfulness of his household. Without intending to hurt Oyone's feelings, he stupidly remarks: "Of course, it isn't simply because they have money. They have children too. Why, even a poor household would be cheerful so long as there were children about." Oyone is deeply hurt but says nothing until late that evening when they are lying in bed.

Seeing that her husband was still awake, Oyone began to speak to him: "You said that it's lonely without children, didn't you?"

Sōsuke could remember saying something of the sort. But he had not meant to remind Oyone particularly of their own unhappy condition. It was difficult for him to think of a suitable reply. "I was not talking about us," he said.

"But it's because you are always so lonely that you couldn't help saying what you said today. Isn't that so?"

Sōsuke had to admit to himself that there was some truth in what Oyone had said. But for her sake he could not openly say so. Reminding himself that she had only recently been ill, he said jokingly: "Lonely? Of course I am lonely!" But he could not think of anything to say that would be appropriately humorous. He felt helpless. He said simply: "It's all right. You mustn't worry." Oyone remained silent. Sōsuke then tried to change the subject: "There was a fire again last night, wasn't there?"

Oyone then said suddenly, as though in great pain: "I am terribly sorry." She seemed to want to say more, but she became quiet again.[71]

But it is Sōsuke that must endure greater pain. Oyone is a woman, and her husband's love gives her all the security and happiness that she in her humility expects from life. She will never know the kind of loneliness that Sōsuke suffers, for his needs are greater than hers. Besides, Oyone's reliance on Sōsuke is a great strain on him. He must provide all the strength needed by the two, and he fears that unless he finds some source outside himself, he will soon have none left. Finally in desperation, he turns to religion for possible comfort. He must conquer his sense of guilt, loneliness, and helplessness if he and Oyone are to survive.

He takes a short leave from his office and goes to a Zen temple in Kamakura. He tells Oyone that he is going to the resort town for a rest and she believes him. There he stays for a few days and tries sincerely to find peace of mind through meditation. But he has never been a religious man, and it is now too late for him to

71. *Zenshū*, 6: 397–98.

begin to penetrate the profound secrets of Zen. He honestly confesses to the old master his inability to benefit from a stay at the temple and leaves.

> He had come to the gate and had asked to have it opened. The bar was on the other side and when he knocked, no one came. He heard a voice saying: "Knocking will do no good. Open it yourself."
> He stood there and wondered how he could open it. He thought clearly of a plan, but he could not find the strength to put it into effect.... He looked behind him at the path that had led him to the gate. He lacked the courage to go back. He then looked at the great gate which would never open for him. He was never meant to pass through it. Nor was he meant to be content until he was allowed to do so. He was, then, one of those unfortunate beings who must stand by the gate, unable to move, and patiently wait for the day to end.[72]

He returns to Oyone, who is disappointed to see that the holiday in Kamakura has not improved his appearance.

One Sunday not long after his return, he goes to the local public bath and overhears two men discussing the weather. They have each heard a nightingale sing and agree that the song was still rather awkward and unpractised. Sōsuke, when he gets home, remembers to tell Oyone about the nightingales. She looks at the sun streaming in through the glass window and says cheerfully, "How nice! Spring has finally come." The novel comes to an end as Sōsuke replies, "Yes, but it will soon be winter again."

The Wanderer

Sōseki began writing *The Wanderer* (*Kōjin*) in 1912 and finished it in the following year. Its main theme, as is that of *The Gate* and *The Heart*, is loneliness. In *The Gate*, the hero tries to find escape in religion, and fails. In *The Wanderer*, the hero, Ichirō, is driven into a state of near-madness, which only increases his awareness of his own loneliness. And at the end of the novel, we leave him as he lies in exhausted sleep, knowing that he will awaken only to continue to wander in hopelessness.

The narrator of *The Wanderer* is Jirō, Ichirō's younger brother. Ichirō, as we see him through Jirō's eyes, is hardly a sympathetic

---

72. *Zenshū*, 6: 475–76.

figure. It is only towards the end of the novel that we begin to realize, with Jirō, that we have judged Ichirō too harshly.

The first big scene of the novel takes place in a small seaside village near the castle town of Wakayama, where Ichirō, his wife Nao, Jirō, and their mother are spending a short holiday. Ichirō asks Jirō to go out for a walk with him. They come to the grounds of a great temple, and there Ichirō suddenly asks Jirō whether he is in love with Nao. Jirō hotly and truthfully denies that he is, and Ichirō apologizes. Then Ichirō makes an extraordinary request: he wants Jirō to find out for him whether Nao is chaste. Jirō is shocked. He then recovers himself enough to say:

> "Test her chastity! I suggest you forget you ever said such a thing."
> "Why?"
> "Why? It's idiotic, that's why!"
> "What's so idiotic about the idea?"
> "All right, then. It's not idiotic. Let's say it's unnecessary."
> "I am asking you because it is necessary."
> I remained silent for a while. It was unexpectedly quiet where we were. There was not one worshipper to be seen. I looked at the deserted scene and as I thought of us sitting alone in the corner of the grounds, I felt a certain eeriness.
> "How do you propose I test her chastity anyway?"
> "I want you and Nao to go to Wakayama and spend a night there."
> I said impatiently, "What nonsense!" My brother then became silent. I, of course, said no more. The sea reflected the last trailing light of the reddish sun, which would soon disappear beyond the far horizon.
> "So you don't want to go, eh?"
> "No, I don't," I said without hesitation. "You know that I would have done anything else for you."
> "All right, I won't insist. But I will suspect you for the rest of my life."[73]

Finally, the two brothers reach a compromise. Jirō will accompany Nao on a day's trip to Wakayama and will try to discover how she feels about her husband.

The reader cannot tell whether or not Ichirō really doubts Nao's faithfulness. She is a subtle woman, whose reaction to Ichirō's coldness is difficult to fathom. She and Ichirō can never become close, for neither of them is willing to break through the other's remoteness. Nao senses Ichirō's suspicions and yet she does not seem to care. She cannot enjoy married life as it is but she does not try to make it any happier. She has immense pride and in order to retain it, she is subtly cruel to Ichirō. Against her kind

73. Zenshū, 8: 143–44.

of cruelty Ichirō has no defense, for it takes the form of extreme passivity. Later in the novel, he confesses to a friend:

"I hit her once but she remained calm. I hit her again but she still remained calm. I hit her for the third time, thinking that she would fight back, but I was wrong. The more I hit her, the more ladylike she became. . . . Was it not cruel of her to use her husband's anger as a means of showing her own superiority? I tell you, women are far more cruel than we are, despite our physical violence. Couldn't she at least have said something then?"[74]

Nao and Jirō go to Wakayama the following day. Though she is fond enough of her brother-in-law, she is slightly contemptuous of him. She knows that Jirō is afraid of his elder brother and that he has been made uneasy by his brother's suspicions concerning his feelings towards her. She is supposed not to know why she and Jirō have come to Wakayama, but she knows very well that theirs is not an innocent sight-seeing trip.

In a private room in a restaurant, Jirō awkwardly asks Nao to be kinder to her husband. At first she pretends not to take him seriously, but there is no need to maintain her cool exterior before Jirō, and she finally breaks down in tears. It is not Jirō's words that have made her cry; she is simply giving release to her feeling of loneliness which has accumulated throughout her years of marriage.

When she regains her composure, Jirō asks, "Tell me honestly, are you fond of my brother or do you dislike him?" She does not answer his question. Instead, she asks in turn, "Why should you want to ask me a question like that? You don't think that I am fond of some other man, do you?"[75] The significant thing is that she never says she is fond of her husband. We know that she does not prefer another man to Ichirō. But we also learn that Ichirō was not wrong in thinking that he was not loved.

While they are sitting in the restaurant, a big storm breaks. They are told that they cannot go back to the village where they are staying. They are forced to spend the night at a hotel in Wakayama.

Another novelist might have introduced a seduction scene at this point, but not Sōseki. What happens in the hotel room is much subtler. Sōseki does not even tell us that Jirō is tempted to seduce Nao. We are left to guess whether Jirō is truly virtuous or

whether he is merely frightened of his brother. And we are not
sure that Nao would have resisted had Jirō made advances. They
are lying in the dark room, waiting to go to sleep.

The dark sky that I had just seen seemed to be raging in my head. I imagined
the three-storied hotel where my brother and mother were staying being
whirled around in the angry sea. Then I began to think of my sister-in-law
sleeping in the same room. True, we had been forced to stay because of the
storm, but I wondered how I should explain myself to my brother. And I
wondered how I would mollify him after I had made my excuses. But at the
same time, I felt a certain pleasurable excitement at the adventure that my
sister-in-law and I were sharing. And I forgot about the wind, the rain, the
waves, my mother, and my brother. But this feeling of pleasure was soon
replaced by a nameless fear.[76]

Despite the fact that Jirō had no conscious wish to betray his
brother, he has a vague sense of guilt. It is this sense of guilt on
Jirō's part that ultimately justifies Ichirō's suspicion. For Ichirō is
suspicious not because of anything Jirō has said or done; his
suspicion springs from his knowledge of the untrustworthiness of
all men. Nao too, though she is not an unfaithful wife, is contemptuous of Jirō because of his virtuous behavior. If she were
completely chaste, she would never have noticed it. Her last
words to Jirō that night are: "In the last resort, what cowards
most men are."

The next morning they are able to leave Wakayama. Ichirō
receives them coldly. When he and Jirō are alone, he asks him:
"Well, what did you learn about Nao's character?" Jirō answers
abruptly: "Nothing." He realizes immediately, and too late, that
he has been unnecessarily cruel to his brother.

My brother and I did not speak. We looked at each other in silence. It was
painful for me to sit there thus. When I think about it now, I realize how much
greater my brother's pain must have been than mine. Then he said, his voice
shaking a little:
"Jirō, I am your brother. I did not expect such a cold reply from you."[77]

They soon return to Tokyo. They all live in their father's
great house. Tension mounts within the family, and Jirō decides
to leave home and live in a boardinghouse. Even his mother
welcomes his decision, for she hopes that Ichirō's condition will

76. *Zenshū*, 8: 176.
77. *Zenshū*, 8: 190.

improve with Jirō gone. Jirō visits Ichirō in the latter's study and informs him that he is moving out.

"When do you intend to go?" asked my brother.
"I hope to leave this coming Saturday," I replied.
"Alone?" he asked.
I was dumbfounded by this strange remark, and I gazed blankly at my brother's face for a while. I did not know what to say. I could not decide whether he was being intentionally sarcastic or whether he was becoming a little mad.
He had often been sarcastic to me before, but normally his sarcasm was no more than the natural expression of a man whose mind was far keener than that of others around him. I had learned not to resent it, for I knew that he meant no harm by it. But on that particular occasion, his remark hit me very hard.
My brother looked at me and gave a giggle. There was a touch of hysteria in it. "Of course you are going alone," he said. "There's no need for you to take anyone with you."
"You're quite right. I want to live by myself, merely so that I may breathe some fresh air for a change."
"I should like a breath of fresh air too. But there is no place for me in all Tokyo where I can get it."[78]

Ichirō's condition gets steadily worse, until in desperation Jirō asks Ichirō's colleague—they teach at the same college—to induce him to go away for a holiday with him. The friend agrees and finally succeeds in taking Ichirō away from Tokyo. Jirō secretly asks Ichirō's friend to write him a letter if possible, so that he may learn how his brother is progressing. This the friend does, and the last part of the novel is told in his words.

Ichirō finds it impossible to relax anywhere, and they wander from place to place. The friend is a placid and sympathetic man and tries sincerely to help Ichirō out of his unhappy state. Ichirō is less inhibited in his company than he was before, and the friend comes to know him far better than his family ever did.

This is what your brother said. He suffers because nothing he does appears to him as either an end or a means. He is perpetually uneasy and cannot relax. He cannot go to sleep and so gets out of bed. But when he is awake, he cannot stay still, so he begins to walk. As he walks, he finds that he has to begin running. Once he has begun running, he cannot stop. To have to keep on running is bad enough, but he feels compelled to increase his speed with every step he takes. When he imagines what the end of all this will be, he is so frightened that he breaks out in a cold sweat. And the fear becomes unbearable.

I was surprised when I heard your brother's explanation. I myself have never experienced uneasiness of this kind. And so, though I could comprehend what he was saying, I could feel no sympathy for him. I was like a man who tries to imagine what it is like to have a splitting headache though he has never had one. I tried to think for a while. And my wandering mind hit upon this thing called "man's fate"; it was a rather vague concept in my mind, but I was happy to have found something consoling to say to your brother.

"This uneasiness of yours is no more than the uneasiness that all men experience. All you have to do is to realize that there is no need for you alone to worry so much about it. What I mean to say is that it is our fate to wander blindly through life."

Not only were my words vague in meaning but they lacked sincerity. Your brother gave me one shrewd, contemptuous glance; that was all my remarks deserved. He then said: "You know, our uneasiness comes from this thing called scientific progress. Science does not know where to stop and does not permit us to stop either. From walking to rickshaws, from rickshaws to horse-drawn cabs, from cabs to trains, from trains to automobiles, from automobiles to airships, from airships to airplanes—when will we ever be allowed to stop and rest? Where will it finally take us? It is really frightening."

"Yes, it is frightening," I said.

Your brother smiled. "You say so, but you don't really mean it. You aren't really frightened. This fear that you say you feel, it is only of the theoretical kind. My fear is different from yours. I feel it in my heart. It is an alive, pulsating kind of fear." [79]

On another occasion the friend tries to convince Ichirō of the necessity for religious faith, though he himself has never felt a need for it.

"Try not to think of yourself as the center of life," I said to your brother. "Forget yourself and you will become more relaxed."

"What, then, do you suggest I rely on instead?"

"The gods," I said.

"What are they?" he asked. . . . If I remember correctly, the conversation continued as follows:

"Since the world does not move in accordance with your wishes," I said, "you have no choice but to admit that there is some will outside of yourself at work."

"I do admit that."

"And don't you think that this will is much greater than you?"

"It probably is since I am always the loser. But most men I see are more evil than I, more ugly, more faithless. Why should I suffer defeat at their hands? The fact is, I do. That's why I become angry."

"But you are talking about the rivalry that exists between men. I am talking about something much greater."

"What exactly is this vague thing that you are talking about?"

"If it doesn't exist, then you won't be saved."

"All right. Let's assume that it exists."

"Leave everything in its care; let it guide your life. When one is on a rickshaw, one falls asleep, trusting the rickshaw man to lead one safely to wherever one wants to go."

"I know of no god that I can trust as much as I can a rickshaw man. You really feel the same way as I do, don't you? This sermon you've been giving me, you don't believe any of it. You've made it up simply for my benefit."

"You are wrong."

"Really? You make no attempt to assert your own self?"

"Quite so."

My uneasiness increased as your brother continued to press me. But it was too late for me to try to change the course of the conversation. Then your brother suddenly raised his hand and slapped my face.

As you know, I am a rather insensitive person. I have therefore managed to live so far without quarrelling with anyone or giving anyone cause to be angry with me. Possibly because I was placid, my parents never laid their hands on me when I was a child or, needless to say, when I had passed my childhood. I had been slapped for the first time in my life, therefore, and I could not help the sudden anger that I felt.

"What do you think you're doing?" I said.

"See?" your brother said.

I could not quite understand his meaning. "Rather violent, aren't you?" I said.

"See? You have no faith in the gods, have you? You do become angry, after all. A little thing like a slap upsets your equilibrium. Where's your self-possession?"

I said nothing. Indeed, I could not think of anything to say. Your brother then suddenly stood up. My ears were filled with the heavy sound of his feet as he ran down the stairs.[80]

There is really nothing that Ichirō's friend can do or say to help him, for he cannot answer the question that Ichirō asks of him one day as they are walking down a mountain. "What is it that brings your heart and my heart together? And what is it that finally parts them?"

The friend ends his letter saying:

At the time I began writing this letter [some days ago], your brother was fast asleep. And as I am about to come to the end of it, he is once more in deep sleep. . . . There is somewhere in me the feeling that he would be fortunate if he were never to awaken. But at the same time, I feel that it would be terribly sad if his sleep were to last forever.[81]

80. *Zenshū*, 8: 392–95.
81. *Zenshū*, 8: 422.

The Heart

The Heart, perhaps the most loved of Sōseki's later novels, appeared in 1914, two years before the author's death. It is divided into three parts and is told, with great simplicity, in the first person all the way through. The narrator of the first two parts is a young student who befriends the main character, Sensei, and that of the last part is Sensei himself. The young man remains nameless throughout; and so does Sensei, for "sensei" is not really a name but a word that is close in meaning and usage to the French "maitre." In fact, none of the other important people in the book have names. Sensei's best friend, whom he betrays, is referred to simply as "K," and the girl they both fall in love with as "Ojōsan," or "Mademoiselle." Such reluctance to give his characters names perhaps suggests that Sōseki intended *The Heart* to be an allegory of sorts. And indeed, the lyrical simplicity of the entire book has rather a parable-like quality. It is as though Sōseki wished here to strip his story of the intellectual and psychological complexity of his earlier works, and write with the intensity of a lyrical poet. For this reason perhaps, *The Heart* is a beautiful book; but it is also much more innocent than its predecessors.

The young man first sees Sensei, a man some years older, on the beach at Kamakura, where they are both vacationing. He sees him again the next day, and the next. He is bored, for he is in Kamakura alone, and finds himself attracted to the aloof-seeming stranger. At last they speak to each other, when the young man helps Sensei find his spectacles in the sand. And so their friendship begins.

> The next day, I followed Sensei into the sea, and swam after him. When we had gone more than a couple of hundred yards out, Sensei turned and spoke to me. The sea stretched, wide and blue, all around us, and there seemed to be no one near us. The bright sun shone on the water and the mountains, as far as the eye could see. My whole body seemed to be filled with a sense of freedom and joy, and I splashed about wildly in the sea. Sensei had stopped moving, and was floating quietly on his back. I then imitated him. The dazzling blue of the sky beat against my face, and I felt as though little bright darts were being thrown into my eyes. And I cried out, "What fun this is!"[82]

But this is the last time he expresses such simple joyousness. As he continues to see Sensei after they return to Tokyo, the brightness slowly fades away from his life; and though the world around him does not lose its beauty for him, it becomes gray and tranquil, and rather sad—as if the older man had begun to cast his shadow on his young friend's life.

> We sat still for a moment or two, as though made immovable by the silence around us. The beautiful sky began slowly to lose its brightness. And before us, the delicate, green maple leaves, which looked like drops of water just about to fall from the branches, seemed to grow darker in color. From the road below, the sound of cart wheels reached our ears. I imagined that a man from the village had loaded his cart with plants or vegetables and was on his way to some fair to sell them. Sensei stood up, as though the sound had aroused him from his meditation.
> "Let us go home," he said.[83]

Throughout their relationship, Sensei maintains a certain distance between himself and his young friend. He is not unkind, but there is a forbidding air about him always, which persists even in his behavior towards his wife, a gentle and lonely woman. But despite Sensei's aloofness, the young man continues to seek his company. For him, the association is perhaps, as Sensei suggests, only a phase in his preparation for manhood and love. And the time will come, Sensei tells him, when he will drift away. "I felt a strange kind of sorrow when he said this. 'Sensei, if you really think that I shall drift away from you, there is nothing I can do about it. But such a thought has never crossed my mind.' "[84] All Sensei is saying is that people change; but the young man in his innocence does not understand.

He is quite unaware that his own attachment to Sensei is indeed an example of human fickleness. For he has become fonder of Sensei than of his father, a decent but limited country gentleman. And when summer comes and he must go home, he is very reluctant to leave Sensei, even though his father is ill.

He goes to see Sensei once more before he goes away. He cannot know that this is the last time they will ever see each other.

> I said goodbye and stepped out of the house. Between the house and the outer gate, there was a bushy osmanthus tree. It spread its branches into the night as if to block my way. I looked at the dark outline of the leaves and thought of

83. *Zenshū*, 9: 69.
84. *Zenshū*, 9: 33.

the fragrant flowers that would be out in the autumn. I said to myself, I have come to know this tree well, and it has become, in my mind, an inseparable part of Sensei's house. As I stood in front of the tree, thinking of the coming autumn when I would be walking up the path once more, the porch light suddenly went out. Sensei and his wife had apparently gone into their bedroom. I stepped out alone into the dark street.[85]

The second part of the novel describes the young man's stay in his country home. It may appear to be a digression, for here the central figure of the novel, Sensei, remains very much in the background. Indeed, even the young man begins to seem secondary to his father, whose chronic kidney ailment has taken a turn for the worse, and who lies in bed slowly dying. Yet this part is quite pertinent to Sōseki's overall intention. The old man is in almost every respect different from Sensei: he is secure in his conventionality, he has children, and there is a simple warmth in his relationship with his wife. And it is by contrast to his condition that Sensei's becomes all the more poignant.

My father, when he came out of his delirium, seemed to want everybody by his side so as not to feel lonely. He would want my mother most of all. He would look around the room, and if she was not there, he would be sure to ask, "Where is Omitsu?" Even when he did not say so, his eyes would ask the question. Often, I had to get up and find her. She would then leave her work, and enter the sickroom saying, "Is there anything you wish?" There were times when he would say nothing, and simply look at her. There were also times when he would say something quite unexpectedly gentle such as: "I've given you a lot of trouble, haven't I, Omitsu?" And my mother's eyes would suddenly fill with tears. Afterwards, she would remember how different he used to be in the old days, and say, "Of course, he sounds rather helpless now, but he used to be quite frightening, I can tell you."[86]

But in the end, Sōseki seems to be saying, even this old man cannot escape the bitterness of human fate; for as he is about to die, he is deserted by his son.

One day a letter comes for the young man from Sensei. The young man is harried, for his father clearly has little time left; and after only a cursory glance at the long letter he puts it down on the desk. But as he does so, a sentence near the end catches his eye: "By the time this letter reaches you, I shall in all likelihood be dead." He rushes back to his father's room, and is told that his condition has improved slightly for the moment.

85. *Zenshū*, 9: 85–86.
86. *Zenshū*, 9: 123–24.

Once more, I returned to my room. I looked at my watch, and began to examine the railway timetable. I then stood up, rearranged my dress, and putting Sensei's letter in my pocket, went out through the back door. As though in a nightmare, I ran to the doctor's house. I wanted to ask the doctor whether my father would last another two or three days. I wanted to beg him to keep my father alive for a few days more, by injection or any other means in his power. The doctor was unfortunately out. I had not the time to wait for him. In any case, I was too agitated to stay still. I jumped into a rickshaw and urged the man to hurry to the station. . . . The noise of the engine filled my ears as I sat down in the third-class carriage. At last, I was able to read Sensei's letter from beginning to end.[87]

By committing this desperate, unconventional act in his forlorn hope to see Sensei before he kills himself, he has cut himself off from his family. They surely will never forgive him, and he will never forgive himself. And like Daisuke in *And Then—*, or Sōsuke in *The Gate*, or indeed like Sensei himself, he will live the rest of his life as a lonely outsider.

Sensei's letter, which forms the last part of the novel, is ostensibly an attempt to explain his life to his young friend; but it is really not so much of an explanation as an expression of the lonely man's desire to try once and for all to communicate with another human being. Sensei himself knows that it is a vain wish. "You and I belong to different generations, and so we think differently. Of course, it may be more correct to say that we are different simply because we are two separate human beings."[88]

Sensei's narrative begins when, as a young man about to go to university in Tokyo, he loses both his parents. His family also is country gentry, and as the only heir, he is left with a sizeable inheritance. His uncle, who has political ambitions, becomes his guardian; and very soon, he begins to speculate secretly with his nephew's money. Sensei discovers this only after he has gone to Tokyo. By that time, it is too late: most of his inheritance has disappeared.

I was incredibly naïve to have trustingly left everything under my uncle's management. It depends of course on the point of view: some, who do not consider worldliness a great virtue, may admire such a display of innocence. At any rate, I can never think of those days without cursing myself for being so trusting and honest. I find myself asking, "Why was I born so good-natured?"

87. *Zenshū*, 9: 129–30.
88. *Zenshū*, 9: 249.

But, I must admit, I sometimes wish that I had never lost my old innocence, and that once more I could be the person that I was.[89]

It is this unfortunate incident early in his life that twists his character, and prepares him for the act of treachery that he himself will commit. The theme that Sōseki has been obsessed with throughout his later career—that of betrayal, guilt and loneliness —now begins to unfold itself with stark simplicity.

While at the university Sensei decides to move out of his noisy boardinghouse and rent a room in some respectable household. He is offered a room at the home of an army officer's widow, and moves in there. The lady has an attractive daughter, Ojōsan. And of course, he falls in love with her.

Sensei has one very good friend at the university, whom he calls "K." K, born the second son of a well-to-do priest, is now the adopted son of a doctor, who has sent him to university on the understanding that he too will become a doctor. But K, a fanatical devotee of the ascetic life, has made up his mind to be instead a student of philosophy and religion. His foster father, when he discovers this, is furious, and disowns him. His real father reluctantly, and only in the most formal sense, admits him back into the family; but he too is furious, and refuses to have anything more to do with him. K, now without family or money, becomes more eccentric and high-principled than ever. Sensei writes:

I said to him that he should do no more work than was necessary, I told him that for the good of his own great future, he should rest and enjoy himself. . . . But he insisted that scholarly knowledge was not his only objective. What was important, he said, was that he should become a strong person through the exercise of will-power. Apparently, this could be done only by living in strait-ened circumstances. Judged by ordinary standards, he was perhaps a little mad.[90]

And later he adds:

Having grown up under the influence of Buddhist doctrines, he seemed to regard respect for material comfort as some kind of immorality. Also, having read stories of great priests and Christian saints who were long since dead, he was wont to regard the body and the soul as entities which had to be forced asunder. Indeed, he seemed at times to think that positive mistreatment of the body was necessary for the glorification of the soul.[91]

89. *Zenshū*, 9: 148.
90. *Zenshū*, 9: 177–78.
91. *Zenshū*, 9: 180.

Unable to stand aside and watch his friend starve any longer, Sensei finally persuades him to move in with him. It is a terrible mistake; for K, in spite of all his principles, falls in love with Ojōsan. And Sensei, too insecure and suspicious of others to believe that she would have no interest in such an odd fellow as K, is consumed by jealousy, and becomes mean and cunning. He sees that K's puritanical self-regard has made him extremely vulnerable to ridicule, and proceeds systematically to destroy him. One day he goes out for a walk with his unsuspecting friend, and in a deserted park, after listening to him talk of his painful love for Ojōsan, begins to taunt him with reminders of his past aspirations.

I walked by K's side, waiting for him to speak again. I was waiting for another chance to hurt him. I lurked in the shadows, so that I might take him by surprise. I was not an ignorant man, and I was not without conscience. Had a voice whispered into my ear, "You are a coward," I might at that moment have returned to my normal self. And had the voice been that of K, I would surely have blushed with shame. But it was not in him to admonish me. He was too honest, too simple, and altogether too righteous to see through me. I was in no mood to admire his virtues, however. Instead, I saw them only as weaknesses.

After a while, K turned towards me and addressed me. . . . He was taller than I, and so I had to look up at him. I was like a beast of prey, waiting to spring.

"Let us not talk about it any more," he said. I was strangely affected by the pain in his eyes and in his words. For a moment, I did not know what to say. Then, in a more pleading tone, he said again: "Please, don't talk about it." My answer was cruel. The beast sank its teeth into the victim's throat.

"Well, so you don't want me to talk about it! Tell me, who brought up the subject anyway? If I remember rightly, it was you. Of course, if you really want me to stop, I will. But not talking about it isn't going to solve the problem, is it? Can you will yourself to stop thinking about it? Are you prepared to do that? What's become of all those principles of yours that you were always talking about?"

K seemed to shrivel before my eyes. He seemed not half so tall as he once was. As I have said before, he was a very stubborn fellow; but he was also too honest to ignore his own inconsistency when it was bluntly pointed out to him. I saw the effect my words had had on him, and I was satisfied.[92]

Having demolished his rival, Sensei immediately goes to the widow and asks permission to marry her daughter. She agrees. But before Sensei can bring himself to tell K about the engagement, the widow innocently mentions it to him.

Ridiculed and now betrayed by the only person he has trusted, K has little left to live for. Even his principles, which he believed to be so important, have proved to be worthless dreams. Two days after hearing the news, he kills himself. There is no accusation in the suicide note he leaves his friend. It asks simply that Sensei notify his relatives and take care of his body. But the last line, added perhaps as an afterthought, is full of anguish. It is the cry of a man who has for too many years been alone: "Why did I wait so long to die?"[93]

Time and again over the years, I wondered what had caused K to commit suicide. At first, I was inclined to think that it was disappointment in love. I could think of nothing but love then, and quite naturally, I accepted without question the first simple and straightforward explanation that came to my mind. Later, however, when I could think more objectively, I began to wonder whether my explanation had not been too simple. I asked myself, "Was it because his ideas clashed with reality that he killed himself?" But I could not convince myself that K had chosen death for such a reason. Finally, I became aware of the possibility that K had experienced loneliness as terrible as mine, and wishing to escape quickly from it, had killed himself. Once more, fear gripped my heart. From then on, like a gust of winter wind, the premonition that I was treading the same path as K would rush at me from time to time, and chill me to the bone.[94]

What finally destroys Sensei, then, is not so much his guilt as the loneliness that comes with it. His guilt is an obsession which he cannot share even with his wife; it is like a prison wall, which shuts him in and all others out.

But perhaps in the end, he is more fortunate than Sōsuke or Ichirō, or Kenzō, the hero of the novel that Sōseki would write next. For as he writes his letter to his young friend in the quiet of the night, resolved at last to make his escape, his agonized heart seems to find some peace.

Considering my situation, I am really quite calm. Even the sound of street-cars, which seems to become audible only when the rest of the world has gone to sleep, I can hear no more. The forlorn singing of the insects reaches me through the closed shutters, and one feels that their song is of the dews of coming autumn. My wife sleeps innocently in the next room. The pen in my hand makes a faint scratching sound as it traces one character after another down the page. My heart is tranquil as I sit before my desk. If the strokes of the characters seem sometimes ill-arranged, you must not think this due to my mental state. Attribute it, rather, to my inexperience with the pen.[95]

93. Zenshū, 9: 233.
94. Zenshū, 9: 244.
95. Zenshū, 9: 137.

Grass on the Wayside

Grass on the Wayside (*Michikusa*), Sōseki's only autobiographical novel, was written in 1915. He was forty-eight then, and suffering from severe stomach ulcers. Next year, before he could complete *Light and Darkness* (*Meian*),[96] he died.

The period that the novel deals with is very short; it begins soon after the author's return from London in 1903, and ends as his writing career is about to begin. (*I am a Cat* was published in 1905.) Kenzō (the name Sōseki gives himself) is at this time in his middle thirties, and his wife in her middle twenties.

One guesses that it was at about this time that relations between Sōseki and his wife became strained and he began to be acutely conscious of his isolation. And in writing about this period of his life more than a decade later, and a year before he died, he was perhaps trying to express once and for all his sense of failure as a man and his bitterness at having been betrayed even in his childhood; and he perhaps wanted to say that whatever his career as a novelist might have been, his personal life had been an irrelevance, like a weed growing forlornly on the side of the road.

The novel is a description of a man's loneliness, his need to be loved by his wife and his perverse rejection of her love, and his feeling of betrayal by all that he had at one time or another needed. It is an expression of a man's anger at all the scars that he received

96. This novel, which is considerably longer than *The Heart* or *Grass on the Wayside*, has been much admired by some Japanese critics. It is not discussed in this essay, however, mostly because it is unfinished and, despite its length, leaves the reader quite at a loss as to where the author might eventually have taken him. Also, it is the most tedious of Sōseki's later novels. Its main characters are a self-centered and really rather uninteresting young businessman and his equally self-centered wife, whose dealings with each other, their friends and relatives are described in great detail. The two seem fond enough of each other, but we are not sure whether the young man really loves his wife, and neither is she. He had been in love, we learn, with another girl, who had suddenly and without explanation married some other man. The novel stops as the hero meets his old sweetheart at a resort. Exactly what significance this meeting is intended to have in the scheme of the novel, we cannot know.

Light and Darkness has admirers in Japan presumably because Sōseki's examination of character is more meticulous and perhaps more complex here than in any of his other novels. But it lacks passion. There is not a line in it that touches one. The trouble is that Sōseki seems not to care very much about any of the characters in the novel. And because of the detachment, or the indifference, the technical virtuosity that he displays often has the effect of pedantry.

It is as though all the poetry and the passion that was in Sōseki was spent at the end of *Grass on the Wayside*. And so I feel that I should end my essay on him with that novel rather than with the unfinished *Light and Darkness*.

as a child, and at his own inability to escape from his enslavement to the past.

It is through Kenzō's chance encounter with his former foster father, Shimada, whom he has not seen for many years, and the old man's subsequent insistence upon renewing their old association, that the past, which he has tried to delete from his consciousness, once more forces its way into his life.

Kenzō, as a child of two, had been given away to this man and his wife, Otsune. And when the couple were divorced—Kenzō was about eight then—he had been returned to his real parents. But for ten years after that, Kenzo had continued to see Shimada periodically, and remained nominally his foster son. This is how Kenzō remembers the time he was returned to his original home:

> To his father he was simply a nuisance. He would look sometimes at the boy as though he could not quite understand how such a mistake had been made. Kenzō was hardly a child to him; rather, he was some animate object that had wandered uninvited into his household. And the love that was in Kenzō's expectant heart was brutally pulled out by the roots and left to wither in the cold. . . .
>
> With too many children to take care of already, Kenzō's father was very reluctant to assume any responsibility for him. He had taken the boy back only because he was his son; he would feed him, but he was not going to spend a penny on him if he could help it. After all, he had thought that the boy was off his hands for good.
>
> Besides, Shimada saw to it that Kenzō remained legally his adopted son. From his father's point of view, then, Kenzō was a bad risk; for what was the point of spending money on the lad when Shimada could come and take him away any time he wished? I'll feed him if I must, was his attitude; but let Shimada take care of the rest—it's his business.
>
> Shimada was no less selfish. He was content to stand by and allow the situation to continue as long as it suited him. They won't let him starve, he assured himself; when he's old enough to earn some money, I'll get him back, even if it means going to court.
>
> Kenzō had no home, either in the sea or the hills. A wandering creature that belonged nowhere, he found his food sometimes in the water and sometimes on land.
>
> To his father and to Shimada both, he was not a person. To the former he was no more than an unwanted piece of furniture; to the latter, he was some kind of investment that might prove profitable at a later date.[97]

Shimada, soon after the chance encounter, sends in a request to Kenzō through a middle man, Yoshida, that he be allowed to

97. *Zenshū*, 9: 483–84.

visit him. Reluctantly, Kenzō agrees. He feels contempt for the
old man, but in his contempt there is guilt.

He remembered that he and Shimada often went out boating, accompanied
by a boatman always dressed in the traditional straw skirt. When they were
some distance from the land the boatman would cast his net, and Kenzō would
watch the gray mullet with their silver scales dancing frantically as they were
brought to the surface. Sometimes the boatman would take them three or
four miles out and catch gilthead. On such occasions the boat rocked so much
that Kenzō could hardly keep awake. He enjoyed himself most when a swellfish
got caught. As it puffed up in anger Kenzō would tap it with a chopstick as
though it were a drum.

Such childhood memories began to haunt him continually after his interview
with Yoshida. They were fragmented, but they were vivid nonetheless; and
always Shimada figured in them. He realized, with surprise and pain, that so
much of what he remembered was associated with the man.[98]

Shimada soon begins to visit Kenzō at regular intervals. At
first he is respectful—after all, Kenzō is a professor—and formal;
but very quickly he becomes brutally familiar, and discloses his
real purpose in coming to see Kenzō. He needs money.

It is the story of this renewed relationship between Kenzō and
Shimada that forms the core of the plot. But the main intention
of Sōseki is to describe his own loneliness and the tragedy of his
marriage as they are revealed through the appearance of Shimada,
and perhaps to ask for understanding of himself as an extension of
the unloved child.

Because of Shimada, Kenzō must once more have close dealings
with his relatives, who are his elder brother Chōtarō, his elder
sister Onatsu, and Hida, her husband. For he must first of all try
to find out from them what are Shimada's true circumstances,
whether he does indeed need money. And if things get too
unpleasant between himself and Shimada, he will need their
intercession. Moreover, Shimada has already gone to Hida with
the preposterous suggestion that Kenzō become his adopted son
again.

These three people are all years older than Kenzō. Chōtarō is a
humble clerk in a government bureau, and Hida an accountant
in some obscure firm. They all depend on Kenzō for support,
moral if not financial, for he is the only "successful" man in the
family. To them he appears rich, and a trifle arrogant. They

cannot know that Kenzō finds them an unbearable burden on his conscience. They all belong to the past, not only in Kenzō's mind but in fact; they are twilight people, with only night awaiting them. "They all carried with them the stink of decay. And his life was tied to theirs by blood and a shared past."[99] He feels no affection for them, for they too have betrayed him in the past.

Kenzō had had another brother, between him and Chōtarō in age, who had died of an illness. On several occasions during his illness this brother had shown Kenzō his silver hunting watch and said, "I am going to leave you this." And for almost two months, young Kenzō had greedily dreamed of the day when he would be able to hang his first watch on his sash. How impressed and envious the others would be!

When the brother died, his widow honored the promise and announced to the family at large that the watch would go to Kenzō. Unfortunately, the watch was then lying in a pawnshop; and of course, Kenzō had not the means to redeem it. All he had inherited, therefore, was merely the right to have it if he could.

Some days later the family gathered together again. Without warning, Hida brought out the watch and put it down ceremoniously in front of Chōtarō. It was beautifully polished—Kenzō had never seen it so shiny—and tied to it was a new silk cord with a piece of coral at the end. "This is for you," Hida said. "That's right," said Kenzō's sister, "it's for you." "How very thoughtful of you," Chōtarō said. "Thank you very much."

Silently Kenzō watched the three, who seemed hardly aware of his existence, and kept his bitter thoughts to himself. He hated them for the way they had insulted him; and as he watched them gaily chatting away, seemingly unmindful of all the hurt they had caused, he could not help wondering why they had chosen to treat him so cruelly.

And so he had sat through the meeting not saying a word, not asserting his claim to the watch nor demanding an explanation. He had expressed his disgust through silence. And in the end he had found satisfaction in the thought that there was no worse punishment for his brother or his sister than to be despised by someone of their own blood.[100]

Kenzō knows his judgement of them is harsh, and his own bitterness towards them makes him ashamed; but he cannot help it. And as he now watches his brother, once so irresponsible and selfish, leading a life more forlorn than his own, he feels only a detached kind of pity. Yet the following passage, where Sōseki describes with seeming coolness his brother's condition, contains deep emotion—not so much sadness for his brother, as suppressed anger at all the misery that surrounds him.

99. Zenshū, 9: 310–11.
100. Zenshū, 9: 508–9.

Chōtarō was a lowly civil servant, and worked in a large government office in the middle of Tokyo. That he should have pursued his pathetically insignificant career for so long in this magnificent building seemed to him incongruous. "There are plenty of young, eager fellows around," he would say. "Who has any use for a decrepit character like me?"

Several hundred men worked like slaves night and day in the building. His own energy was about to run out; and like a shapeless shadow in the midst of all the furious activity, he somehow managed to drag out his existence. By nature inclined to indolence, he secretly hated work. He was sickly, and already he was dried up like an old man. Every morning he would leave for his office, his face drawn and without color, as though he were going to his death. "Having to stay up so many nights is ruining me," he would say. He caught cold easily, and was always coughing. Sometimes he would feel feverish; and he would be frightened, thinking that perhaps he had tuberculosis.

The sort of work he did would have been hard even on a vigorous young man. Every other day he was put on night duty. After having worked through the night he would stagger home in the morning almost unconscious. All that day he would lie exhausted in bed, without the will to do anything. But he made himself go on, so that he and his family could survive.

In all the years of his service, he was never promoted. He was simply a piece of machinery installed in a corner of the office; it would tick away until it wore out. Sometimes Kenzō would look at this man, seven years his senior, and uncharitably think to himself: "Surely in the twenty-five years he's worked there, he might have done something that attracted attention."

In his youth, the man had been quite different. He had been a rather gay type. He had no time for books, and would spend his time learning to play some musical instrument or other, or cooking a dish that momentarily caught his fancy. That he had been a wastrel in his youth, he was wont to admit to others: "You might say I'm paying for my sins now."

Through the death of older sons, he became the heir. When their father died, he immediately sold the family property, and with the proceeds paid off his old debts. He then moved into a small house. The contents of the old house that he couldn't get in there, he sold also.

Eventually he became the father of three children. The eldest daughter was his favorite. In her adolescence this girl became seriously ill with tuberculosis. He did everything in his power to save her, but to no avail. When after two years of illness she died, everything he owned was gone. In his wardrobe, there was not one respectable item of clothing left. The carefully tended suit that he now wore to the office was one that Kenzō had worn constantly while abroad.[101]

His sister is a pathetic, shabby woman in her early fifties, a victim of chronic asthma. She is uneducated, and rather vulgar. "She was a great talker. Moreover, there was not a hint of breeding in her speech. After a few minutes of her company

101. *Zenshū*, 9: 336–38.

Kenzō would invariably become silent and disapproving. And he would tell himself bitterly, 'This woman, alas, is my sister.'" [102]

Everybody knows that her husband, Hida, keeps a mistress. It is rumored that she was once a low-grade prostitute. This, Kenzō finds easy to believe, for Hida is in no condition to afford better. He is totally callous towards his wife, and on those rare occasions when he is at home, he ignores her as she lies coughing and wheezing her life away in the next room. Yet, even when this sad woman speaks of her dead baby, Kenzō is unmoved.

She bored Kenzō even more when she talked about her dead child. He had never seen the baby, alive or dead. "Let's see, what was his name?" "Sakutarō, it was," she said, and pointed at the small buddhist shrine on the wall. It seemed not only appropriately gloomy inside but quite dusty. From where he sat, it was impossible to make out the posthumous names engraved in gold on the black memorial tablets. But he was not going to get up to find out. "I suppose the small one is his." "That's right. We decided that the normal size wouldn't be quite right for a baby."

His face stayed expressionless. His second daughter had once almost died of dysentery, but not even the memory of his own suffering at the time could make real for him his sister's loss.

She pulled her gaze away from the shrine and said, "At this rate, I might be joining them soon." Kenzō deliberately looked away. [103]

These people, then, are ghosts from the past, who bring degrading reminders of all the pathos of Kenzō's boyhood. And in trying to find a dignified and meaningful life all his own, a life that is somehow quite disconnected from the past, he makes the mistake of demanding too much of the present. In his way he loves his wife, and she loves him. But his demands are too great, and she cannot meet them. As a result, there comes to exist a seething resentment between them.

Kenzō has never learnt to give love, for as a child he was never given the chance. His only way of expressing love, then, is to demand it; and this often takes the form of self-pity.

The following Sunday he stayed in his house. At about four in the afternoon he had a hot bath, in the hope that this might change his mood. He felt surprisingly relaxed when he came out. He lay down on the floor, and fell into a very deep sleep. When his wife came in to announce dinner, he was still lying there like a man in a coma.

He went to the table feeling refreshed, but as soon as he sat down, he began to feel a slight chill down his back. He sneezed violently, twice. His wife, sitting

102. *Zenshū*, 9: 261.
103. *Zenshū*, 9: 422–23.

beside him, said nothing. Neither did he; but he resented her lack of concern. She remained silent, hating his pride and reserve, and thinking: it's his fault that I can't behave like a wife.

Later that evening he decided he had a cold. He knew he should go to bed early, but work kept him up till midnight. The rest of the family had all gone to sleep. Had his wife been awake, he would have asked for some hot gruel to make him sweat. Resignedly he crept into his cold bed. He felt thoroughly chilled, and at first found it difficult to go to sleep. But he was much too exhausted to stay awake for long.

When he awoke the next morning, he felt surprisingly rested. He wondered whether he had shaken the cold off after all. In the bathroom, however, the usual rub-down with cold water proved a great ordeal. Every muscle in his body seemed to have gone limp. Martyr-like, he forced himself to appear at the breakfast table. He could not enjoy the food. He had only one bowl of rice instead of the usual three. He put a pickled plum in his empty bowl, then poured hot tea over it. Noisily and ostentatiously he began to sip the brew. Had he been asked why he was doing this, he would have been at a loss for an answer. His wife watched him quietly. Again he became irritated at her aloofness, which seemed particularly calculated this morning. He coughed loudly two or three times for her benefit. But she was quite unmoved.[104]

His wife wishes to understand him, but she cannot. She has the limited understanding of a middle-class woman who has had a happy childhood, and she cannot imagine the damage that her husband's loveless childhood has done to his proud nature. His self-pity therefore is simply contemptible in her eyes, and his aloofness an indication of callousness. His inability to respond openly to her innocent gestures of affection, she takes for contempt on his part for her childishness. She does not know that he is simply frightened of such gestures, afraid that if he were to respond, somehow the only protection he has ever had—aloofness—would go.

The only affection ever shown him as a child had come from his foster parents. Even that had been a devouring, possessive affection, more an expression of their general greediness than anything else; and it had frightened him.

The couple were inwardly uneasy about Kenzō, and constantly demanded reassurances of affection from him. On cold winter evenings as they sat huddled around the brazier they would ask him: "Who is your father?" And Kenzō would point at Shimada. "All right, who is your mother?" Kenzō would look at Otsune and point. The interrogation would not yet be over; only partially satisfied, they would go on to ask: "But who are your real father and mother?" Kenzō, with obvious reluctance, would once more point his finger at one and then the other. Somehow this gave the two pleasure, and they would smile happily at each other.

There were periods when the scene was enacted almost every day; and there were also times when they were not satisfied with this simple interrogation. Otsune was the more persistent of the two. Sometimes she would ask, "Where were you born?" And Kenzō would have to describe the house that he could even now remember—the little house with the red gate and the grove. His answers were of course mechanical, since Otsune had seen to it that they would be precisely what she wanted to hear. But this did not seem to detract from her pleasure at hearing them repeated. "Whose child are you really? Come on, tell me the truth." It was a terrible ordeal for Kenzō. Sometimes he felt more anger than pain, and would stand stiff as a board, refusing to answer. But Otsune would simple-mindedly decide that his silence was due to his boyishness; she did not know how much he hated her at such times.

The couple did everything in their power to make Kenzō exclusively theirs. They regarded him no doubt as their possession by right. And the more they pampered him, the more possessive they became. He did not mind so much being owned physically; but even his childish heart grew fearful at the thought of becoming emotionally enslaved to them.

They were always careful to make him conscious of their generosity. He was never allowed to eat a cake or wear a new kimono without being told that it had come from "your father" or "your mother." They seemed not to know that such desperate efforts to win his gratitude would only make him resentful.

Every time he was reminded of what "your father" or "your mother" had done for him, he would immediately want to escape their clutches and be on his own. And he very quickly trained himself to dissociate his favorite toys from the people that had given them to him. The toys had to have an independent existence; otherwise how could he enjoy them?[105]

And now, even an act of kindness on Kenzō's part towards his wife goes sour in the end, for it is inevitably accompanied by a defensive churlishness. One day he discovers to his horror that she has been pawning some of her clothes to supplement her meagre housekeeping allowance.

He made up his mind to work harder and earn more money. Not long afterwards he returned home with some extra money in his pocket. He pulled out the envelope containing the bills and threw it down in front of his wife. She picked it up and looked at the back to see where it had come from. Neither of them said a word.

Her expression was blank. I could have shown pleasure, she thought, only if he had said something kind. Kenzō, on the other hand, resented her seeming indifference, and blamed her for his own silence. The money would help them satisfy their material needs. As a means of bringing warmth to their relationship, it was quite useless.

105. *Zenshū*, 9: 353–55.

Kenzō's wife could not bear to think that the money had brought them so little pleasure. A couple of days later she showed him a length of cloth and said: "I thought I would make you a kimono. How do you like it?" She was smiling cheerfully.

Kenzō doubted her sincerity. She thinks she's being clever, he told himself; she's not going to fool me with her bogus charm. Chilled by his attitude, she quickly left the room. As he watched her leave, he thought unhappily: I have been forced somehow or other to behave like this to my wife.[106]

His children are afraid of him. He knows that it is his fault, but he cannot help resenting it. He has alienated them by his own bad temper, but not knowing how to make amends, he tries to relieve his guilty conscience by further acts of violence.

His irritability was such that sometimes he thought he would go mad unless he gave vent to it. Once for no reason at all he kicked a pot of flowers that belonged to the children off the verandah. It was a prize possession of theirs, something their mother had bought them after days of begging on their part. The sight and sound of the red pot smashing as it hit the ground gave him some satisfaction. But when he saw the broken stem and the torn flowers, he was momentarily overcome with sadness at the useless, cruel thing he had done. These pitiful flowers, he thought, had seemed beautiful to the children; and now their own father had destroyed them.

He felt some remorse; but he could not bring himself to go to the children and confess. And there was the usual rationalization that he could fall back on: "It's not my fault—it's hers. If I act like a madman sometimes, it's because of her."[107]

Shimada's intrusion on their lives makes Kenzō and his wife move even further apart. She understands neither the revulsion nor the guilt that he feels towards his former foster father; nor why, despite his obvious dislike of the old man, he continues to give him money that they can ill spare. Kenzō's behavior strikes her as irrational, as another manifestation of his perverseness.

Her lack of understanding is to be expected, since Kenzō will not tell her much about his past. Perhaps to do so would somehow make him more vulnerable; perhaps he is afraid that to share his pathetic memories with her would make *him* seem pathetic in her eyes.

Yet, for all Kenzō's—or Sōseki's—hostility towards his wife, no woman in Japanese fiction is treated with greater understanding than she is. Here is how Sōseki describes her soon after she has had her baby:

106. *Zenshū*, 9: 303.
107. *Zenshū*, 9: 394.

It was her custom to complete her morning toilet after she had seen her husband off to work. That morning again she sat forlornly before the mirror, gazing at all the hair that had come out with the combing. Losing blood at childbirth had not affected her half so much. Every time I bear a child, I give a part of myself away—such was her feeling. It remained vague in her mind, for she was not used to articulating her feelings. Yet no matter how faintly recognized, it brought with it a sense of accomplishment, and at the same time resentment. Either way, it increased her love for the newborn child.[108]

Kenzō knows his wife is worth a great deal more than Shimada and the others; he knows that she has offered him love as no one else has ever done; but what he knows is twisted out of existence before it is ever expressed in deed or word. And in his self-destructive way, he allows the bitterness he feels towards those who have wronged him to spill over and corrode the only love he has known.

Kenzō's association with Shimada comes to an end when Shimada's insatiable greed at last exhausts his patience. And with this final ugly encounter between the two, this phase of Kenzō's life too is ended. The New Year is approaching, Shimada says, and he has certain obligations; might Kenzō spare "a hundred or two"?

Kenzō never felt less sympathetic towards the man. "I don't have that kind of money," he said.

"You can't fool me. I know very well you've got money to spare. Look at this house."

"Think what you like. I'm telling you I don't have it because I don't."

"All right, let me ask you this: is it true you get eight hundred yen a month?"

It was incredible. More shocked than angry, Kenzō said, "What I make is my business—it has nothing to do with you."

Kenzō's answer was apparently not quite what Shimada had expected. Not being half so bright as he was impudent, he was now at a loss as to how to handle his opponent. After a brief pause he said, "So you won't help me, no matter how hard up I am?"

"That's right. I won't give you a penny."

Shimada stood up and walked out of the room. As he stepped out of the house and was about to close the front door behind him he turned around and looked up at Kenzō, who stood silently in the hall. "I'll never come to this house again," he said. His eyes shone in the dark. Without uneasiness or fear Kenzō stared back. The disgust and anger he felt afforded him ample protection against the other's hatred.[109]

108. *Zenshū*, 9: 467.
109. *Zenshū*, 9: 481–82.

Later, through another middle man, Kenzō agrees to give
Shimada a hundred yen. And in return his relatives obtain for him
a written guarantee that Shimada will never trouble him again.

The guarantee means nothing to Kenzō. He knows he was not
obliged to see his former foster father in the first place. Shimada
never had any legal claims on him, and all he will have to do in
the future is simply refuse to see him, guarantee or no guarantee.
As he watches his relatives congratulating themselves on the
happy outcome of the unpleasant episode, he is filled with sadness.
They have no idea what pain his recent association with Shimada
has brought him, what guilt and disappointment, what sense of
barrenness.

The Shimada episode is indeed over. But what came with it
will always remain with Kenzō. Such things will happen again,
only to remind him of his own loneliness.

Thus *Grass on the Wayside* ends. In all that Sōseki wrote,
nothing is so terrible or despairing as these last lines:

"What a relief," Kenzō's wife said with feeling. "At least this affair is
settled."

"Settled? What do you mean?"

"Well, we have his signed statement now, so there's nothing to worry about
any more. He won't come here again. And even if he does, all you have to do is
tell him to go away."

"But that's how it's always been. If I had wanted to, I could have told him
to go away a long time ago."

"But we didn't have anything in writing before. We do now, and that makes
a big difference."

"So you're relieved, eh?"

"Certainly. It's all settled now."

"But it isn't, you know."

"Why?"

"It just seems so on the surface, that's all. Of course, women like you who
take formalities very seriously would think otherwise."

There was anger and skepticism in her eyes. "All right then, what else has to
be done before it really is?"

"Hardly anything in this life is settled. Things that happen once will go on
happening. But they come back in different guises, and that's what fools us."
He spoke bitterly, almost with venom.

His wife gave no answer. She picked up the baby and kissed its red cheeks
many times. "Nice baby, nice baby, we don't know what daddy is talking
about, do we?" [110]

110. *Zenshū*, 9: 515–16.
6—T.J.N.

Tōson

Shimazaki Tōson was born in 1872 in the village now known as Misaka Magome in Nagano Prefecture.[1] His given name was Haruki, and he was the fourth son of Shimazaki Masaki. "Tōson" is his pen name. The Shimazaki family had for generations held the hereditary post of *shōya*, or village headman; and in the days when Magome, as it used to be called, was a station—it stands on the old Nakasendō, one of the five great highways of the Edo period—their house was the *honjin*, or officially designated stopping place for daimyo and other dignitaries travelling to and from Edo. They were a prominent local family, therefore; and though they were not samurai, they belonged to that literate, land-owning rural upper class which formed, in the Edo period, a kind of country gentry.

In 1881, Tōson was sent to Tokyo to study. There he lived for a while with his elder sister and her husband, and later with friends of theirs. He lived with the latter, a family named Yoshimura, for some ten years. He spent all of his adolescence in Tokyo, then, without much contact with his father or mother. His father visited him once, in 1884, and after a brief stay in Tokyo returned to Magome. Before they could see each other again, the father died in 1886. This was the man that Tōson was to write about in his last completed novel, *Before the Dawn* (*Yoakemae*). That his years of growing up in Tokyo were a difficult and lonely time for him, Tōson makes clear in his novel, *When the Cherries Ripen* (*Sakura no mi no juku susu toki*).[2] The family he lived with were kind to him, but they were after all not his own. Perhaps his early sense of homelessness had something to do with the almost obsessive consciousness of family that we find in some of his novels.

---

1. The main facts of Tōson's life are listed chronologically in *Shimazaki Tōson zenshū* 19 vols. (Tokyo, 1948–52) (hereafter referred to as *Zenshū*), 18: 647–68. A book that contains useful factual information is Senuma Shigeki, *Hyōden Shimazaki Tōson* (Tokyo, 1959).

2. This was completed in 1917. It is the only novel of Tōson's that is not discussed in this essay.

While still a boy Tōson developed a serious interest in English. In 1887, he entered Meiji Gakuin, where, he had been told, English was taught well. Meiji Gakuin was a Christian institution, an excellent example of its kind, and it offered much that was new and exciting to the impressionable middle-class youths that went there. What concerns us here is not so much the Christian doctrine to which these students were exposed, as the atmosphere of emancipation that must have pervaded the academy. Their reaction to this atmosphere may embarrass us now, for it was inclined to be excessively sentimental and naïve. The sound of chapel bells, the sweet music of the hymns, the enthusiastic and not very enlightened discussions of English Romantic poetry in the dormitory, the calf love cherished by the boys for the girls (these latter were from Meiji Jogakkō, a school closely associated with Meiji Gakuin) whom they would see filing into the pews— all these made up a world which was remarkable for its immaturity.[3] But with the naïveté came a new self-awareness, a consciousness of the importance and dignity of one's feelings, which Tōson tried later to express in those rather sentimental lyrics of his early career as a poet.[4]

Tōson graduated from Meiji Gakuin in 1891. It was soon afterwards that through the encouragement of Iwamoto Yoshiharu,

3. This period of Tōson's life is described in detail in *Sakura no mi no juku suru toki*.
4. Kamei Katsuichirō seems convinced of the direct influence of Christianity on Tōson's early poetry. He does indeed point to a remarkable instance of Tōson's borrowing from a Japanese Christian hymn. Here, in translation, are the first two verses of the hymn, which was published in 1888:

> When the sun sets, in the stillness
> I shall pray,
> And forget for a while
> The cares of this world.

> With head bowed, in the shade of a tree
> Where none but God
> Will hear me,
> I shall repent my sins.

And here are two verses, again in translation, from Tōson's "Disappearing Stream" ("Nigemizu"), which was included in his *Collection of Young Leaves* (*Wakanashū*), published in 1897:

> When the sun sets, in the stillness
> I shall dream,
> And forget for a while
> The cares of this world.

> There, in the shade of the flowers,
> Where none but you
> Will know,
> I shall weep for love.

See Kamei, *Shimazaki Tōson-ron* (Tokyo, 1954), 30-32.

who was then editor of *Jogaku Zasshi*, he began his career by publishing in that journal popular pieces with such titles as "Beaconsfield's Wife," "The Poet Milton's Mother," "The Poet Byron's Mother," and "The Heroines in George Eliot's Novels."[5] In 1892, he joined the staff of Meiji Jogakkō as a teacher of English. In the following year, he became associated with the new literary journal, *Bungakkai*. The dominant personality of the group that formed around this journal was Kitamura Tōkoku (1868–94), the erratic but gifted essayist and poet who was also teaching at Meiji Jogakkō.[6]

In 1896, he left Tokyo for Sendai in the northeast to teach at Tōhoku Gakuin. The suicide of Kitamura Tōkoku in 1894, which seems to have affected Tōson deeply, had left the *Bungakkai* group without a leader; and we gather from Tōson's second novel, *Spring (Haru)*, which deals with the period immediately preceding the author's departure for Sendai, that life in Tokyo had ceased to have any attraction for him. Perhaps he felt that his years of literary apprenticeship—which is all his activities with the *Bungakkai* amounted to—were at last over, and that he was ready to work alone. At any rate, during his year's stay in Sendai, he put together his first collection of verse, *A Collection of Young Leaves (Wakanashū)*, which immediately established him as a young poet of great promise. "In *Young Leaves*," he wrote later, "I tried to express in verse my feeling that at last, in Sendai, the dawn had arrived."[7]

These poems may strike the modern Western reader as being at best rather unoriginal. But what may seem to us today undistinguished lyrical verse—and here we are speaking merely of the content, not the language—can very easily have seemed novel and exciting to the Japanese public of 1897. Tōson himself was very conscious of having done something new. He suggests that he had tried to give new meaning to those Japanese words which had become shopworn in their traditional setting;[8] and indeed,

---

5. These are all to be found in *Zenshū*, 1. They are, as one might guess, of little literary worth.

6. Francis Mathy has written three excellent studies of him: "Kitamura Tōkoku: The Early Years," *Monumenta Nipponica*, vol. 18, nos. 1–4 (1963), pp. 1–44; "Kitamura Tōkoku: Essays on the Inner Life," *Monumenta Nipponica*, vol. 19, nos. 1–2 (1964), pp. 66–110; and "Kitamura Tōkoku: Final Essays," *Monumenta Nipponica*, vol. 20, nos. 1–2 (1965), pp. 41–63.

7. *Zenshū*, 14: 94.

8. *Zenshū*, 14: 322.

it would seem that such words as *koi* (love), *haru* (spring), *tabi*
(journey), and *tabibito* (those that journey) gained a certain freshness under Tōson's handling.[9] In verse which was surprisingly
free and flowing, he used these words to express the sentiments of
modern Japanese youth. "I went to Sendai," he tells us, "and
there tried to make poetry come closer to the hearts of young
people like myself." [10]

It is extremely difficult to point with any precision to those
qualities of sentiment which made Tōson's poetry "new." One
can only hope, by reference to such words as "nostalgia,"
"heartache," and "loneliness," to convey an approximate idea
of what they are. True, similar feelings are present in the haiku
of Issa (1763–1827).[11] But what is significant is that Tōson found
it necessary, and Issa did not, to escape from the confined, implicit
world of traditional verse to the more flexible, explicit world of
song. And in the very explicitness of the emotionalism of Tōson's
poetry, we find a new kind of self-consciousness and, unavoidably
perhaps, a new sentimentality which we do not find in Issa's
poetry. In "Pillow of Grass" ("Kusamakura"), for example,
which is one of the most successful of the poems in *Young Leaves*,
the melancholy of the poet comes very close to seeming in our
eyes a pose. But we find it expressed with that freshness which is
characteristic of Tōson's best lyrics; and this freshness comes from
the young poet's genuine sense of discovery of a new world of
poetic articulation. Here, in translation, are a few verses from
"Pillow of Grass":

> I am like the morning cloud
> That brought rain the night before;
> Or I am like the evening rain
> That tomorrow will be a floating cloud.
>
> Like leaves that have fallen
> I was carried by the wind;
> And with the clouds of the morning
> Came over the river at night.
>
> Perhaps here, in Miyagi Plain,
> In this ancient wilderness without a path

9. See Kamei, *Shimazaki Tōson-ron*, p. 43.
10. *Zenshū*, 14: 315.
11. Tōson found Issa an essentially modern poet for this reason. See *Zenshū*, 15: 50.

> I shall cease to wander,
> And find some rest.
>
> The grass has withered under the northern sun;
> And in this barrenness of Miyagi Plain
> My troubled heart
> Shall find a home.
>
> In loneliness I listen to the northern wind;
> To my ears it is like the sound of the harp;
> And to my eyes the stones
> Are like flowers in bloom.[12]

One of the great weaknesses of the poetry in *Young Leaves* is its small emotional range. Of this Tōson himself was quite aware. In his essay, "Diction and Poetry" ("Gagen to shika"),[13] Tōson complains of the limitations of sound and of vocabulary inherent in the Japanese poetic language, which must necessarily limit the variety of moods the poet may express. That Tōson should therefore have moved on to fiction is not altogether surprising. It would seem that no matter how hard he tried, he could not entirely break away from the restrictions imposed upon him by long-established poetic usage. For one thing, his ear had been attuned to the seven- and the five-syllable counts; and for another, he could not materially increase his vocabulary without violating his sense of proper poetic diction. In other words, with almost the same tools that the seventeenth-century poet Bashō, for example, had used in his brief, suggestive poems, Tōson tried to bring to his own some of the range and explicitness of Western poetry. He was not altogether unsuccessful; there is in such a work as "Pillow of Grass" a sustained lyricism which is rare in Japanese poetry, and for this alone he deserves to be ranked amongst the most important of modern Japanese poets. But to Tōson, endowed as he was with great descriptive power, poetry must have come to seem very confining. Some years later, shortly after he wrote his first novel, he remarked: "I write novels because they are the best medium for what I want to say.... There seem to be quite a few people in Japan today who have

12. *Zenshū*, 2: 24–25.
13. *Zenshū*, 2: 377–91.

turned from poetry to prose; I suppose they found they could not express themselves satisfactorily in verse."[14]

It may occur to the reader later that there is a world of difference between Tōson of *Young Leaves* and Tōson of *The House* (*Ie*) or of *Before the Dawn*. But actually there is not as sharp a separation between these phases of his career as may be imagined. There is of course a difference. First, the author of *The House* is more mature than the author of *Young Leaves*; and second, one literary form, such as the novel, may bring out certain qualities in a man which another form, such as lyrical verse, may not. But this is not to say that the "romantic" poet is suddenly transformed into a "realistic" novelist. The passionate lyricist in Tōson always remained. However conspicuous in his novels the labored detachment of his technique may become, we always sense the painfully suppressed emotionalism that lies beneath the surface; and what gives his sometimes heavily written novels their peculiar power is the seemingly incongruous presence of the poet in the background.

In 1897, he resigned from Tōhoku Gakuin and returned to Tokyo. Poetry was his main interest until 1899. Then in April of that year, he left Tokyo for Komoro, a small town in one of the central provinces, Shinshū, to teach at Komoro Gijuku. The same month he married a girl who had graduated from Meiji Jogakkō. They remained in Komoro until 1905; and it was while living as an impoverished schoolteacher in this remote castle-town that Tōson began to write prose seriously. Here he wrote his remarkably mature *Chikuma River Sketches* (*Chikumagawa no suketchi*), which is a collection of impressionistic pieces describing the local scene;[15] a series of short stories, "The Old Head of the Household" ("Kyūshujin")[16] being the first of these to be published; and a part of his first novel, *Broken Commandment* (*Hakai*). "In Sendai," Tōson said later, "I found some of the peace that my troubled spirit so needed; in Komoro, I found even greater peace."[17]

---

14. *Zenshū*, 17: 304.

15. This was published much later in 1911–12.

16. This is a rather contrived story concerning the infidelity of a pretty Tokyo woman married to a dull, middle-class provincial much older than herself. It is narrated by their maid, who betrays her mistress to the husband. It is a self-conscious piece of storytelling, crudely conceived, and seems to belong to that school of realistic writing which seeks a shortcut to realism by the choice of such themes as marital infidelity. It has little resemblance to Tōson's novels, either in style or kind of content.

17. *Zenshū*, 18: 651.

Broken Commandment

Tōson began writing this novel in 1904 in Komoro and completed it in the following year after he had resigned his post there and moved back to Tokyo. It was with this novel that he hoped to launch his career as a fully committed professional writer. "I passed some years as a teacher," he tells us, "and in my free time was a student of literature; but eventually I came to realize that I was regarding the matter of vocation too lightly and decided that it should coincide with my inner ambition."[18] The novel, when it came out in 1906, was an immediate success, and Tōson's future as a full-time writer was assured.[19]

Whatever differences of critical opinion regarding this first novel of Tōson's we may find among literary historians, there seems to be agreement on one point: namely that it constitutes a landmark in the history of modern Japanese realism. Indeed, whether or not we agree with the view that a new literary school —that of "naturalism"—was founded with its publication, we cannot deny that in *Broken Commandment* we find less melodrama and contrivance than in the works of those writers who had dominated the Japanese literary scene until the rise of such men as Tōson and Sōseki.

The hero of the novel is a young *eta*[20] by the name of Segawa Ushimatsu. By keeping secret the fact of his unusual birth he has managed to go through the prefectural normal college in Nagano without mishap, and is now a schoolteacher in the fair-sized town of Iiyama, which is also in Shinshū. The main theme of the novel is concerned with the strain this deception places on

18. *Zenshū*, 14: 69–70.

19. See Hirano Ken, *Gendai sakka-ron zenshū*, 2: *Shimazaki Tōson* (Tokyo, 1957), pp. 23–40.

20. The *eta*, with the *hinin*, were two outcast groups during the Edo period, set apart by law from the ordinary commoners or *ryōmin*. The *eta* were placed higher than the *hinin*; however, while it was possible for a *hinin* to become a commoner or for a commoner to become a *hinin*, the *eta* class was strictly hereditary, and its members had no hope of ever joining the ranks of commoners. The *eta* engaged in occupations which were generally regarded with distaste, such as assisting in executions and working with hides. They were forced to live in separate communities and were forbidden to have normal social intercourse with commoners. In 1871 the *eta* ceased to be an officially separated class. However, prejudice against them is still noticeable, especially in central and western Japan.

In early editions of the novel, the words *eta* and *shinheimin* (new commoner) are used. However, in the *Zenshū*, the *eta* are more delicately referred to as *buraku no hito* (those from the settlement). Compare, for example, *Zenshū*, 3: 6 with *Hakai* (Tokyo, 1906), p. 4.

Ushimatsu and his decision finally to confess his secret. The title *Broken Commandment* refers to Ushimatsu's breaking of his father's commandment, which was that he must never tell anyone of his eta birth.

Unfortunately the title tends to mislead the reader into assuming that the moral issue at stake for Ushimatsu is whether or not he should disregard his father's admonishment. But what makes *Broken Commandment* such a remarkable book for its time is the complexity of Tōson's handling of Ushimatsu's psychology. We find as we read the novel, that Ushimatsu's deception springs from motives far less conventional than the mere desire to obey his father. We begin to see quite clearly that though the consideration of filial obedience is indeed real enough for Ushimatsu, it becomes also a means of rationalizing his own fears of censure and ostracization. It is the presence of this added dimension in the interpretation of the protagonist's motives that makes *Broken Commandment* an essentially modern and historically important novel. The presence or absence of social consciousness in it does not seem to me to be a problem of great relevance. Tōson is more interested in Ushimatsu the eta than in the eta class as a whole.[21]

The novel begins rather crudely. In less than ten pages Tōson tells us, with much explicitness, almost all we need to know about Ushimatsu's background and his present dilemma. We learn that he is an eta schoolteacher who has so far succeeded in arousing no suspicion regarding his origin; that he is at the same time a fearful and secret admirer of the works of Inoko Rentarō, who, because he too was an eta, had been forced to resign his post as teacher at the prefectural normal college and is now courageously writing polemical works asserting his self-respect as an eta; that he, Ushimatsu, has just decided, out of fear, to move from his present lodgings at an inn to a room in a local temple, because another eta, a guest from out of town, has been asked to leave the inn; and that his father, now a cattle-herder in a distant mountain pasture in the same prefecture, had some years ago admonished him never to divulge his origin if he wished to have a respectable place in society. Moreover, the title of the novel alone leaves no

21. Maruyama Shizuka, for example, takes Tōson to task for not relating the sufferings of his eta hero to a larger framework. Itō Shinkichi, on the other hand, praises *Hakai* for its social consciousness and mentions the fact that the Soviet translator considered Tōson "the greatest figure in modern Japanese literature." See Maruyama, *Gendai bungaku kenkyū* (Tokyo, 1956), p. 282; and Itō, *Shimazaki Tōson* (Tokyo, 1947), p. 144.

doubt in the reader's mind that Ushimatsu's secret will eventually come out in the open.

The introduction, then, is rather too explanatory: it tells us too much too quickly. However, the manner in which Tōson begins his novel implies something about his intention. The bare outline of the story is in itself of little consequence to him. What he wants to do is to write a modern psychological novel, where the essential thing is not the situations themselves, but the way in which they affect the behavior of the protagonist; where Ushimatsu's pathetic behavior does not seem to be the result of accidents which, in the normal course of things, he might well have avoided, but the necessary result of his being an intelligent eta, with certain characteristics peculiar to him, placed in a series of situations which in themselves are not extraordinary. This means that the success of *Broken Commandment* depends to a large extent on whether or not the author manages to convince the reader that given the peculiar characteristics of Ushimatsu and the initial set of circumstances in which he is put, the outcome of the plot is natural. Judged in this light, *Broken Commandment* is not entirely successful, for it collapses in the end in a heap of tasteless melodrama; nevertheless, the restrained realism that is characteristic of most of the novel represents a considerable achievement.

Perhaps the most impressive aspect of the novel is the inconspicuous way in which Tōson depicts, through a series of minor incidents which gradually increase in tension, Ushimatsu's fear of discovery and his growing sense of shame and self-contempt at his own life of deception. Such a scene as the following, which takes place early in the novel, is an example. Ushimatsu has just moved into his room in the temple after witnessing the ejection of the eta from the inn. A fellow teacher at the school and also his best friend since their normal college days, Tsuchiya Ginnosuke, and another fellow teacher, Katsuno Bumpei, pay him a visit.

Ginnosuke and Bumpei followed Ushimatsu up the dark stairs. The autumn sun shone into the room through the leaves of the gingko tree outside, casting a yellow glow on the faded wallpaper, the hanging scroll, and the books and the magazines piled up in the alcove. The window was open, and the chilly air that came in gave even this shabby priest's room a certain freshness. Lying conspicuously on the desk was a copy of Inoko Rentarō's *Confessions*. Ushimatsu pushed it away, not wanting his visitors to see it; and as though to hide his confusion, he quickly went to the cupboard, and saying he had no cushions to offer, produced some blankets.

Ginnosuke looked around the room and said: "You certainly are fond of moving, aren't you? I suppose it becomes a habit. But surely, the room at the inn was better than this?"

Bumpei too was curious. "Why did you move?" he asked.

Ushimatsu tried to seem casual as he said: "It was such a noisy place, you see—"; but his nervousness showed.

Ginnosuke seemed not to notice. "Of course," he said, "if it's quiet you want, you'll certainly get it here. By the way, what was all this business about an eta being thrown out of the inn?"

"Yes, yes," Bumpei chimed in, "I've heard about it too."

Ginnosuke continued: "Maybe the incident upset you? Maybe the inn came to have unpleasant associations for you after that?"

"What do you mean?" Ushimatsu asked.

Ginnosuke laughed. "Well, you must admit you're a little more touchy about such things than I am. Just the other day, I read a story in a magazine about a certain neurotic. Apparently, someone decided he didn't want his cat any more, and left it outside this neurotic's house. It upset the neurotic very much. He just couldn't stand to live in the house any longer. Without even consulting his wife, he went and found another house, and moved. . . . Now, I am not saying that you are like this fellow. But in all seriousness, you're not looking too well these days. There is something the matter with you, isn't there? That's why when I heard about the eta at the inn, I immediately thought of the neurotic and the cat and wondered whether you hadn't decided to move for some such silly reason as that."

"Don't be a fool," Ushimatsu said and laughed loudly; but somehow his laughter sounded forced.[22]

Despite his fearfulness, however, Ushimatsu is emotionally incapable of carrying on his deception with a clear conscience. He is perhaps cowardly, but he is not a schemer by nature. Towards an eta boy at the school who is friendless, he cannot help showing compassion: one day, during a doubles tennis match in which both the teachers and the pupils take part, he rushes onto the court to partner the boy when he sees that no one else will. Immediately after the game is over, however, the ignoble side to his nature once more gains control. He quickly leaves the playground, and finding a spot where he can be alone, begins to brood over his own rashness. His admiration for Inoko Rentarō, despite his attempt to hide it, had already been noticed by his colleagues; no doubt they are talking too of his leaving the inn so soon after the expulsion of the eta. And what will they say now

about his quixotic behavior on the tennis court? Suppose—and
the thought fills him with terror—someone, putting two and two
together, comes to a conclusion about his origin? "The prodding,
cruel afterthought," writes Tōson, "as always pursued him."[23]

It is with the events following the sudden death of Ushimatsu's
father that the action of the novel properly begins. At school one
day, Ushimatsu receives a telegram from his uncle saying that his
father has suddenly died. He goes to the principal immediately.
The latter has no choice but to grant his subordinate a leave of
absence. He does not like Ushimatsu, whom he would very
much like to see replaced by Katsumo Bumpei, who happens to
be the district school inspector's nephew. But he is a wily soul,
and is outwardly very solicitous. He even offers to advance
Ushimatsu some money. "'Don't hesitate to ask if you need any.
After all, you don't want to find yourself short.' He said this with
practised cunning, but to Ushimatsu's ear, the words rang false."[24]

Ushimatsu goes back to the temple, packs his things, and sets
off for his uncle's house, which is in another part of the prefecture.
He walks some miles to the nearest railway station, and there, he
unexpectedly sees Inoko Rentarō, whom he has met once before.
The eta writer recognizes Ushimatsu and is pleased to see his
young admirer. He is accompanied by his wife and a lawyer by
the name of Ichimura. Ushimatsu learns that Ichimura is a candidate in the coming election for the Diet and that because of his
championship of the underprivileged, Inoko has decided to
accompany him on his campaign tour and give him whatever
support he can. They will be travelling part of the way with
Ushimatsu.

As Inoko leaves the train with his two companions, he promises
to visit Ushimatsu at his uncle's place in the small town of Netsu,
since it is included in their itinerary.

The coach became suddenly very quiet. Ushimatsu closed his eyes, and
leaning his head against the iron pillar by his side, began to think about his
unexpected encounter with Inoko. It was perhaps unreasonable, but he could
not help feeling a little dissatisfied. Despite Inoko's informality and friendliness,
Ushimatsu thought he sensed a certain reserve in the older man. How was it,
he wondered to himself, that he could not communicate the respect and love
he felt for him? And though without bitterness, he felt a twinge of envy towards
Ichimura, who seemed so close to Inoko.

23. *Zenshū*, 3: 70.
24. *Zenshū*, 3: 79.

It was then that at last Ushimatsu was able to face the truth about himself. He saw that the respect, the sympathy, all that drew him to Inoko sprang from the one pitiful fact that he, Ushimatsu, too was an eta. Everything else between them was finally irrelevant. So long as he kept this one fact a secret, how could he hope to touch the other man's heart? He thought: "How wonderful it would be if I could just tell him! Would he not then grasp my hand and say joyfully, 'You too!' "[25]

And so, for the first time in his life, Ushimatsu makes up his mind to tell a stranger what he really is. The introduction of Inoko in the novel immediately after the death of Ushimatsu's father has therefore a symbolic purpose. The two opposing forces within Ushimatsu himself—the fear of discovery and the desire to admit openly his true identity—are externally represented by the father and the eta writer. And the final decision of Ushimatsu's to confess is thus also the victory of what Inoko represents over what the father represents. The problem, however, as treated by Tōson is not a simple moralistic one. He is not opposing deceitfulness, say, to truthfulness. Neither Ushimatsu's father nor his uncle is represented as being dishonest. Indeed, they are very decent people, whose only concern is that they be allowed to live with dignity. But they are old-fashioned and thoroughly conventional, so that the only means they have of escaping prejudice is to lie about themselves and thus by implication accept its validity. And so they had left the eta settlement in the larger Shinshū town of Komoro and moved to Netsu simply in order to disassociate themselves from eta society. Ushimatsu, however, is not like them. He is better educated and more intelligent. Self-respect therefore demands a greater price of him than it ever did of his father or uncle. For the two older men, respectability and self-respect are synonymous. Ushimatsu, on the other hand, learns, largely from Inoko's example, that for an eta whose conscience has been sharpened by an education, they cannot be synonymous. "The uncle," comments Tōson, "simply had no idea what it was that troubled a young man such as Ushimatsu. He was old-fashioned, and he was happy so long as there was no change in his present condition. If the day ended uneventfully, he was content."[26]

Ushimatsu is greeted warmly upon his arrival by his aunt and

25. *Zenshū*, 3: 88–89.
26. *Zenshū*, 3: 131.

uncle, who have no children of their own. The uncle tells him
that his father was fatally wounded by a bull that had gone wild.
He then goes on to recount how he had managed to reach his
elder brother's lonely hut in the nearby hills before he died and
what the dying man had said:

"I asked him if there was anything he wanted to say. He was in pain, but I
tell you, his mind was as clear as ever. 'For a cattle-herd like me,' he said, 'this
is as good a way to die as any. Only one thing bothers me, and it's about
Ushimatsu. I've gone through a lot of hardship, all for his sake. There's something I told him never to do. Just tell him, please, that he mustn't forget.
He'll know.' . . . Your father had one more thing to say: 'I want to be buried
here, understand, in these hills. No funeral in Netsu, please. And don't tell the
eta in Komoro I've died. This is all I ask.' So I said, 'I understand. Don't worry.'
He must have felt relieved when I said this. He looked at me, smiling. There
were tears in his eyes. He didn't say any more." [27]

Even his father's wish to be buried quietly in the hills, Ushimatsu
knows, was for his sake. For had they asked the temple at Netsu
to conduct the funeral, their origin might have been discovered
in the course of the necessary formalities. "Ushimatsu wondered
at the extent of his father's caution," Tōson comments; "and
thought to himself how relentless some men were." [28]

The uncle himself is a subtly drawn figure. He is kind and
loyal, and in his way an extremely honest man. But Tōson does
not allow him to be a wholly admirable figure. When, a few
days after the burial, he hears that Inoko has been to his house
to see Ushimatsu, he says to his nephew with a mixture of
crudeness and innocence:

"It's about this man Inoko. Tell me, wasn't there once a teacher by that name
at the normal college? Was that him?"
"That's right," Ushimatsu answered, gazing at his uncle's face.
"Is that so," the uncle said. "Just as I thought." He then looked around to
see there was no one about, and stuck out his thumb.[29] "I'm told he's this," he
said. "Be careful." [30]

Leaving his uncle, Ushimatsu goes to spend the day with
Inoko. He is more and more drawn to the writer, in whom he
sees the courage and honesty he himself lacks; and he becomes

27. *Zenshū*, 3: 92–93.
28. *Zenshū*, 3: 93.
29. This is a reversal of the more standard gesture of sticking out four fingers and
bending the thumb to indicate an eta.
30. *Zenshū*, 3: 103.
7—T.J.N.

increasingly ashamed of his own deceitfulness. He tries repeatedly to tell Inoko about himself but fails: he cannot overcome the fear that has become instinctive with him.

In the course of their conversation that day, Inoko tells Ushimatsu an unpleasant story about a certain Iiyama politician named Takayanagi, who happens to be a rival of Inoko's friend, Ichimura, and whom Ushimatsu remembers having seen visiting the school. According to Inoko, Takayanagi also has recently come to Netsu, not to campaign, but to marry in secret the daughter of a very wealthy eta by the name of Rokuzaemon. Rokuzaemon's motive in giving away his daughter to such an unsavory character, Inoko says, is obvious. He has all his life tried to be accepted in high social circles and presumably believes that to have a successful politician for a son-in-law will be an asset. Takayanagi, for his part, is ready to marry an eta girl so long as she brings him money, which he badly needs. The marriage, therefore, is no more than a cold-blooded bargain. Inoko is filled with indignation and disgust at Rokuzaemon's abject aspirations and Takayanagi's callousness.

"Try to look at it from the point of view of someone like myself," says Inoko with unconscious irony; "can you imagine anything more insulting than this affair?"[31] Ushimatsu listens passively. Shortly afterwards, he leaves Inoko's hotel.

And so in the end Ushimatsu did not say what he had intended to say.... As he walked towards his uncle's house, he thought of his own conduct and he wanted to cry. To comfort himself, he tried to think of all the reasons why he shouldn't have told him: there was the promise he had made to his father; there was his uncle to consider too; and once he divulged his secret, what was to prevent Inoko from telling his wife, who, being a woman, would then in all likelihood talk about it to someone else? No, once it got started, there would be no end to it. Why should he, he asked himself, force on himself an eta's identity at this point?[32] Hadn't he passed as an ordinary person so far? And wasn't it perfectly reasonable that he should want to go on doing so?

But he knew that these were rationalizations; he was merely trying to cheat himself. He could not, after all, forgive himself for not having told Inoko.[33]

The next day, Inoko and Ichimura leave Netsu. They tell Ushimatsu that they will be coming to Iiyama soon and that they hope to see him there.

31. Zenshū, 3: 118.
32. The passage from this sentence to the end of the paragraph is not in the Zenshū. I have included it in the translation since it is in the original version. See Hakai (Tokyo, 1906), pp. 230-31.
33. Zenshū, 3: 118-19.

Ushimatsu himself leaves Netsu a few days later. On his return journey, while waiting at a ferry-boat station on Chikuma River, he sees Takayanagi, the politician, with his new bride. Having gone first to Tokyo from Netsu, they are now returning to Iiyama. By taking this circuitous route home, Takayanagi hopes to avert any suspicion concerning his bride's background. Ushimatsu tries his best not to be seen by them. He is afraid that the young woman might know him by sight and that she might somehow have heard from her eta connections that he too was an eta. He is thoroughly disconcerted, then, when he notices her throwing furtive glances in his direction from time to time and then turning to her husband to whisper something in his ear.

On the morning after his return to Iiyama, Ushimatsu is awakened by the maid who tells him that he has a gentleman visitor by the name of Takayanagi. Ushimatsu jumps out of bed and begins tidying the room. Out of sheer habit, he picks up Inoko's books that are lying on the floor and hides them in the closet. In nervous anticipation, he goes downstairs to meet the guest.

A strange conversation takes place in Ushimatsu's room. In a tone that manages to be both confiding and threatening, Takayanagi states his purpose. He has reason to believe, he says, that Ushimatsu and he both have something to hide. Distant connections of his wife's have apparently known Ushimatsu's family. It would be embarrassing for him, he says, if stories were to be told about his wife just prior to his election. And of course, he adds, it would be embarrassing for Ushimatsu if similar stories were told about him. Ushimatsu, however, repeatedly insists that he simply has no idea what his visitor is talking about. And when he is asked what the nature of his relationship with Inoko is, he pretends that they are strangers to each other. Finally, in desperation, Takayanagi begins to beg for Ushimatsu's sympathy. For him, politics is not a hobby, he says: it is a means of livelihood. He must win the election, or he will be ruined.

Takayanagi then suddenly moved off the white blanket that had been his cushion onto the bare floor, and bowed formally. He was like a dog asking for pity. Ushimatsu's face was pale as he said: "I wish you wouldn't jump to conclusions."

"Please, say that you will co-operate."

"But do please listen to what I have to say first. I really don't know what you are talking about. What in the world is there that I can tell others about you? After all, I have nothing to do with you."

"But you know there is something—"

"No, I entirely disagree. There isn't a thing I can do for you, and there isn't a thing you can do for me. Why should there be?"

"All right then," Takayanagi said. "What have you in mind?"

"I don't understand."

"I mean, what are you proposing to do?"

"Why, I propose to do nothing, of course. You and I are total strangers. We have absolutely nothing in common." Ushimatsu then laughed, and added: "That's all there is to it."

"Strangers? Nothing in common?"

"I have not once talked about you to others, and there's no reason why I ever should. I don't like discussing other people behind their backs, you know. Besides, this is the first time we've met."

"True enough, there's no need for you to talk about me. And similarly, there's no need for me to talk about you. But somehow, it doesn't satisfy me to leave it at that. I came all this way to see you in the hope that we might have a heart-to-heart talk. I had hoped, too, that I might be of some assistance to you. You might find me useful, you know."

"You are very kind. But there is nothing you can do for me, I'm afraid."

"But surely, you don't mean to pretend you don't know what I'm talking about?"

"You are under some misapprehension, I think."

"Misapprehension? You can't believe that."

"Why not? I simply don't understand your business, that's all."

"Well, in that case, there is little more I can say. Still, I shouldn't have thought an honest talk would have done any harm. Then let me just say this. I'm concerned for our mutual benefit. *Mutual*, you understand. I'll come again, Mr. Segawa. In the meantime, please think over what I've said."[34]

The irony of the situation is that Ushimatsu arouses Takayanagi's enmity not through loyalty to Inoko and Ichimura or dislike of what Takayanagi stands for but through sheer fright. He makes a dangerous enemy of Takayanagi, without even the compensation of self-respect. There is little sentimentality, then, in Tōson's conception of his hero. But of course, Ushimatsu is not really a contemptible figure. He has at least one redeeming feature, in that had he been more calculating, he might have been inclined to think that he would lose nothing by coming to terms with Takayanagi.

Takayanagi also is conceived with some subtlety. Wily as he is, he too is made irrational by his desire to preserve himself.

---

34. *Zenshū*, 3: 164–66.

Furthermore, he is a man who cannot resist the urge to betray simply for the sake of betraying. As soon as he leaves Ushimatsu's lodgings, he begins to spread the rumor that Ushimatsu is an eta. The disclosure of Ushimatsu's secret will avail him nothing; indeed, it may even bring him ruin. But he imagines that since Ushimatsu has lied to him, he must necessarily be working against him; and his immediate recourse is to destroy his new enemy. He tells Katsuno Bumpei, the inspector's nephew, who has had his eye on Ushimatsu's post of senior master for some time; and Bumpei in turn tells the principal.

At the end of one of the corridors, where there was a flight of stairs leading to the second floor, the two met to have their talk. Few students came that way, and it was a comparatively quiet spot. Ushimatsu, the two knew, was busy elsewhere with his students. They stood side by side, leaning against the grey wall.

"And who told you about Segawa?" asked the principal.

Bumpei smiled and said: "You'd be surprised, sir—very surprised."

"I couldn't even begin to guess."

"Well, as a matter of fact, this man asked me not to mention his name. He felt that he shouldn't get involved in a matter that would affect so seriously the reputation of another. But I assure you, he is a thoroughly reliable source of information. Wouldn't you say, sir, that a candidate for the Diet was reliable?"

"A candidate for the Diet?"

"You know who I mean."

"You don't mean the man who recently came back with a bride?"

"Getting warm, sir, getting warm."

"I see. In which case, he probably heard about it while he was travelling around the country. Well, things like that always come out in the end. Let it be a lesson to all of us." The principal gave a sigh. He continued: "It's a bit of a shock, I must say. Segawa an eta! I'd never have believed it."

"To be honest, I was a bit taken aback too, sir."

"But look at his face—there isn't a thing there that would indicate his lowly origin."

"That's why, I suppose, he managed to fool everybody."

"Maybe so, maybe so. At a glance, no one could tell, wouldn't you say?"

"Appearances are misleading at the best of times, sir. But what about his character?"

"I shouldn't have thought you could conclude much from that."

"But Principal, hasn't his behavior in general struck you as a little odd? Observe him carefully next time. You'll notice, for example, that there's a very furtive look in his eyes."

The principal laughed. He said: "You could hardly take that to be proof of his eta birth." [35]

35. *Zenshū*, 3: 170–71.

But he is at heart only too willing to be convinced. Towards the end of the conversation we find him saying: "I always thought there was something strange about Segawa. Why should he behave in that gloomy way of his, if he had nothing to hide?"[36]

There is soon talk among the staff that there is an eta, as yet unnamed, in their midst. But even with certain doom hanging over him, Ushimatsu continues to act as he always has done. When Bumpei sadistically begins to taunt him with sly questions about Inoko, he cannot help lying.

"Segawa, you have some books by that man, don't you? Would you mind lending me one?"

"I'm sorry, I don't have a thing by him."

"Come now, of course you do! You can't tell me that you, of all people, don't have any of his books! You don't have to hide anything from me, you know. Be a good fellow, and say you'll lend me one."

"You're mistaken, I tell you. I say I don't have any because I really don't."[37]

Anxious now to get rid of Inoko's books before someone finds them in his possession, Ushimatsu takes them to a second-hand bookshop and sells them for a paltry sum. They are books that have meant a great deal to him. "When he left the bookshop and began to think of what he had done, he was filled with remorse. In his mind he said over and over again, 'Maitre, Maitre, please forgive me.' "[38]

It is not long before his colleagues begin whispering to one another that the eta among them is said to be Ushimatsu. One night, his friend Tsuchiya Ginnosuke says to him:

"It's because the others see you brooding so much that they are beginning to say stupid things about you. Your behavior is giving them all kinds of mistaken notions, you know."

"What mistaken notions?"

"Well, for example, that you are an eta. What an incredible idea!"

Ushimatsu laughed painfully. "Why should it matter to you whether I am an eta or not?"[39]

The question is not answered. Tōson does not allow Ginnosuke to say that it really does not matter.

36. Zenshū, 3: 173.
37. Zenshū, 3: 185–86.
38. Zenshū, 3: 198–99.
39. Zenshū, 3: 240.

The following evening, upon learning that Inoko has come to
town, Ushimatsu sets out to see him, resolved to tell him the
truth.

> The moon was in the sky. He felt a little lost, coming out as he did so suddenly
> from the sharp yellowish light of the lamp. The feeble light of the moon had
> crept over the roof-tops and was now resting on the snow on the streets. The
> eaves too cast their shadows on the ground. The night mist, like smoke, had
> enveloped the town, and everything appeared distant and desolate. A pale
> darkness—such perhaps was the way to describe the moonlit scene. He began
> to feel a vague sense of dread.[40]

Up to this point, the novel is on the whole intelligent and when
judged historically, perhaps even brilliant. But suddenly, Tōson
seems to lose control, and the carefully constructed edifice begins
to topple over. What has been a very respectable work of modern
realism quickly becomes embarrassingly trite melodrama.

Ushimatsu will never see Inoko alive again. That evening, at a
political rally, Inoko gives a speech in support of Ichimura's
candidacy. Spitting blood from time to time—he suffers from a
chest condition—he denounces Takayanagi and exposes the
circumstances of the latter's secret marriage to the eta heiress. On
his way back to the inn after the speech he is attacked by Takayanagi's hired toughs and is killed. A few minutes later Ushimatsu
arrives on the scene. "Alas," Tōson writes, "Inoko's body was
already cold. How hard it was for Ushimatsu to take final leave
of his mentor! He laid his face against the blood-drained face of
the dead man and exclaimed, 'Maitre, maitre!'"[41]

Inoko's death forces on Ushimatsu the full realization of his
own abject behavior thus far. The next morning he confesses
before his students in class. "Though I may be of such birth,"
he says at the end of his confession, "I do not think that a day
went by when I did not try to teach you to be honorable people.
If only in return for my efforts, then, please forgive me for

---

40. *Zenshū*, 3: 250. I should like to draw the reader's attention to certain stylistic
peculiarities that may be found in this passage. Such sentences as *tsuki wa sora ni atta* (the
moon was in the sky) and *nokibisashi no kage mo chi ni atta* (the shadows of the eaves too
were on the ground) were, because of their terseness and the use of *atta*, quite revolutionary. Also, the use of *kō* (in this way), as in *kyū ni kō uchi no soto e tobidashite miruto* (as he
rushed out of the house suddenly in this way), was an innovation. See Uno Kōji, "Shizen
shugi no michi," in Satō Haruo and Uno Kōji, eds., *Meiji bungaku sakka-ron*, 2 vols.
(Tokyo, 1943), 2: 46; and Masamune Hakuchō, "Shimazaki Tōson," in *Gendai Nihon
bungaku zenshū*, 8: *Shimazaki Tōson-shū* (Tokyo, 1953), p. 436.

41. *Zenshū*, 3: 253.

having deceived you." [42] The students are much moved by the speech. They march up to the principal's office and cause him no end of embarrassment by asking him to keep Ushimatsu on the staff.

In the meantime, however, the eta whom we saw being ejected from the inn early in the novel has asked Ichimura to recommend a reliable young man who might go to Texas with him and help him start a farm. (He happens to be very rich.) Ushimatsu's name is suggested, and of course, he is hired.

Ushimatsu has been secretly in love with Oshio, the adopted daughter of the rector of the temple where he has been lodging. Ginnosuke approaches the girl and urges her to marry Ushimatsu. He points out that Ushimatsu needs all the moral support he can get.

"I don't quite know how to say it," said Oshio blushing. "You see, I've already decided to do as you suggest."

"Are you sure that you are willing to help him?" said Ginnosuke, gazing at Oshio's face.

"Yes." Her reply moved Ginnosuke deeply. Her love, her tears, her resolute courage—all were contained in that single word. [43]

Takayanagi is punished for his part in Inoko's murder, and Ichimura will win the election. Thus the book ends on this incongruously happy note.

Plot resolution must be one of the most difficult problems facing a novelist or dramatist, and the temptation to tie loose threads together at the end by recourse to a timely death or the sudden appearance of a rich benefactor is perhaps much greater than is commonly supposed. All the same, it would seem that Japanese novelists of Tōson's time succumbed to this temptation more easily than did Western novelists of comparable seriousness.

Tōson once made the interesting comment that a striking peculiarity of those Japanese writers who had had unusual insight into reality—such as Sei Shōnagon (tenth–eleventh century) and Saikaku (1642–1693)—was that they all expressed themselves impressionistically. That is, their writings lacked the sustained structure of Western masterpieces. [44] And it would not be too farfetched to infer from this that, at least in Tōson's opinion, this

42. Zenshū, 3: 269.
43. Zenshū, 3: 281.
44. Zenshū, 14: 35, 317.

impressionistic inclination of the Japanese (including himself) made it very difficult for them to conceive a plot which would suffice for a novel-length work without artificiality or contrivance to mar it.

That *Broken Commandment*, for all the achievement that it represented, was made quite imperfect by the intrusion of melodrama towards the end, Tōson must have known. He later said that when writing *Broken Commandment* he had expended too much energy on useless things, and that with the next novel, he would try to write more naturally.[45] What exactly he meant by this remark is not entirely clear; but at any rate, *Spring*, his second novel, has no plot to speak of, and it is more or less a loosely connected series of impressionistically described scenes.

After *Broken Commandment*, Tōson never wrote a novel around imaginary characters again. *Spring, The House, When the Cherries Ripen*, and *A New Life (Shinsei)* are all based, in varying degrees, on autobiographical material; and his last completed novel, *Before the Dawn*, is based on the life of his father. What seems likely is that Tōson simply felt more comfortable, less strained, when writing around his own personal experiences. There are certain writers who, no matter how talented they may be otherwise, seem to find it extremely difficult to avoid banality in imaginary situations. Tōson was perhaps one of these.

Spring

Spring appeared in 1908. It is essentially a lyrical piece in which Tōson tries to capture in retrospect the emotions of his early manhood in the days of the *Bungakkai*. Years later, in 1930, Tōson wrote: "*Spring* is a work full of faults, but even today, when I take it out and read it, I find that there are passages here and there which bring tears to my eyes."[46]

Spring indeed has faults. It is very loosely constructed, the characterizations are thin and motives obscure, and the attitude of the author is often far too uncritical and sentimental. One distinguished critic has remarked, not without justification, that

45. *Zenshū*, 17: 329.
46. *Zenshū*, 15: 249.

its main interest is historical: were it not for the information it contains about Kitamura Tōkoku and the *Bungakkai* group, he says, it would hardly be worth reading.[47]

Spring is nevertheless a significant work for the student of Tōson. For despite its faults, it reflects the author's peculiarities far more clearly than *Broken Commandment* does. Unlike Sōseki, Tōson at his best does not appeal to the intellect. His inclinations are lyrical and impressionistic rather than analytical, and his novels—with the exception of *Broken Commandment*—are singularly lacking in explicitness. When he is successful, he can suggest moods which seem to transcend the presence of the human actors. But when he is unsuccessful, he seems merely inarticulate and ponderously vague, and the characters begin to seem intolerably without form or meaning.

Tōson tells us that it was with *Spring*, and not with *Broken Commandment*, that he began to write in a way he could feel was his own.[48] In other words, *Spring* may be considered an experimental work in which Tōson tried to give his impressionistic leanings free rein. All of his novels—again, with the exception of *Broken Commandment*—are characterized by loose construction and lack of narrative continuity. *The House* and *Before the Dawn* hold together because here there is no mistaking the author's over-all purpose, and the individual scenes, though often disconnected, are in mood and content related to it. The trouble with *Spring*, however, is that it seems to be totally without design, so that in many of the scenes the reader has no idea where he is being taken or precisely what emotional response is expected of him.

The central figure of *Spring* is Kishimoto (Tōson himself), who is in his early twenties. The novel for the most part describes the young man's struggle to overcome his growing sense of purposelessness. Almost as prominent as Kishimoto is his friend and mentor, Aoki (Kitamura Tōkoku), who is twenty-six and married, has a daughter of two, and is supposedly more mature. Aoki too is disillusioned with life and with himself.

Unfortunately, neither these two nor any of the other characters in the book ever seem to come into focus. Scene after scene flashes past our eyes, and we catch glimpses of Kishimoto, Aoki,

47. Masamune Hakuchō, p. 436.
48. *Zenshū*, 15: 249; 17: 323.

and their friends doing and saying various things, but we cannot see the different aspects of their behavior as parts of a whole. The figures not only remain vague outlines—which would perhaps be forgivable—but they become annoyingly unintelligible. Kishimoto sometimes appears insufferably immature, yet we do not know whether the author intends him to be so; Aoki seems often to be striking a pose, and we wonder whether this is Tōson's intention, but of course, we cannot be sure.

As the novel opens we find Kishimoto returning to Tokyo after a sojourn of many months in western Japan. He had left the capital, we gather, because of an unhappy love affair with a girl already engaged to marry another man. It is this hopeless affair and Kishimoto's general disillusionment that give the content of the novel whatever shape it possesses. The girl—her name is Katsuko—is therefore a key figure. Yet we are allowed to see her for only a brief, unilluminating moment or two. We never discover what kind of a person she is, what she looks like, or why indeed Kishimoto finds her so attractive. We infer, from incidental remarks thrown in by the author, that she is of good family, that she has been a student of Kishimoto's at Meiji Jogakkō where he had taught before his abrupt departure from Tokyo, that she is soon to be married to her fiancé, and that she is in love with Kishimoto. But that is about all we know. Here, for example, is Tōson's description of the first encounter that takes place between the two after Kishimoto's return to Tokyo. They meet at the home of a friend of his named Suge, who has kindly acted as go-between.

Kishimoto looked at Katsuko. He had, before the meeting, gone over in his mind the many things that he was going to say to her; but now that she was there, he found himself tongue-tied. Katsuko too seemed ill at ease, as though she felt she ought not, for appearance's sake, to stay too long. That they had once been teacher and pupil was an added obstacle to any easy flow of conversation between them. They were both conscious of the clandestine nature of the interview, which made them behave with even greater formality than usual. Kishimoto, who at the best of times was the sort that would frown with disapproval when he heard tales of indiscreet conduct on the part of some fellow teacher or other, was particularly stiff on this occasion. He could not forget that he had once been Katsuko's teacher. There were things he had brought back from the journey for her, and these he now produced. As Katsuko stood up to go, he promised to see her again; but he felt in his heart that this was not only their first meeting since her engagement but their last.

The rickshaw man was waiting outside the door. Katsuko stood on the doorstep, and looked forlornly at Kishimoto. Not a word passed between them, but each knew what the other felt. At this moment certainly, the two were more than teacher and pupil to each other.[49]

Suge is deeply sympathetic, as indeed are Kishimoto's other *Bungakkai* friends. They take love very seriously and talk constantly to one another about their own innocent love affairs with a curious admixture of pomposity and reticence. Unfortunately, Tōson seems to be asking us to accept their evaluation of their amorous predicaments on its own terms. And no matter how hard we try not to be too sophisticated, we cannot help feeling slightly uncomfortable.

Suge is also in love. We see the girl briefly at the beginning of the novel. Aoki, Suge, and another friend, Ichikawa, meet Kishimoto on his way back from western Japan at an inn in Yoshihara, a small town on the Tōkaido some miles west of the capital. From Yoshihara the welcoming party and Kishimoto then move on to Tōnosawa. They have just been shown to their rooms at an inn there.

The maids at the inn were young and pretty. They looked as though the hot springs had washed away all traces of their country origin. They wore their clothes well and handled the guests with confidence. Two of them now came into the room bearing food and refreshment.

Suge was fanning himself and seemed more cheerful than usual. The maid called Okimi said, "You must be hot," and went behind him and started fanning his back. Otama, the other maid, waited at the table and joined in the conversation. The young men ate heartily, laughing merrily the while.[50]

Shortly after, in a brief and seemingly irrelevant scene, we see Otama, who has just caught Okimi standing aimlessly about in the corridor, giving her a knowing nudge with her elbow. "You beast!" cries Okimi. And this is the last we see of Okimi. We are not likely therefore to be very seriously concerned—though we are very much surprised—when we are told later that Suge is in love with her.

Something strange began to happen inside Suge after he came away from Tōnosawa. . . . Every night now, he would think of Okimi before going to sleep; and he would experience a kind of excitement that was entirely new to him. He was like the grass that has long been buried under the cold winter snow and comes suddenly to life with the coming of the spring.

A new world opened before his eyes; and he looked with wonder at what he saw.[51]

We are not annoyed with Tōson here for writing nostalgically and sympathetically of calf love; rather, we feel merely that he has no right to be making such solemn announcements so suddenly, with so little warning. Suge, after his return to Tokyo, is shown enveloped in gloom and determined to marry the girl despite the anticipated opposition from his family. As for Kishimoto, his hopeless love affair continues to give him pain. But we can hardly be expected to feel much sympathy for the condition of these young men when the author is so reluctant to describe the prelude to this condition or the objects of their distracted love.

Something similar may be said of Tōson's handling of Aoki and his relationship with Kishimoto. We are given to understand that Aoki has considerable intellectual influence over Kishimoto. Yet Tōson does little to explain the nature of this influence. Occasionally, he does indeed allow Aoki to express his thoughts. But in the end we have only a very vague notion of what Aoki stands for. Here is a typical passage in which Tōson summarizes the content of an impassioned speech Aoki makes before his friends. (It is unrelated to what precedes or follows it.)

He argued for the necessity of religion. In Homer, he said, one found the spirit of the gods of ancient Greece; in Shakespeare, the faith of medieval England; and in Saigyō and Bashō, their own personal faith, peculiar to themselves. If the fact that all these men had some kind of religious faith was not recognized, it was because their faith was not identified with ritual, with some established form of religious worship. To say that these men had no faith simply because it took no outward form was to show complete ignorance of the true nature of the spirit of worship. Look at their great capacity for pity, he said, at their sense of tragedy; could not one call this an aspect of faith?[52]

A similar passage is inserted on another occasion, again unrelated to what precedes or follows it.

After the drinking had begun, Aoki became deadly serious and in a tone of deep indignation began to attack those who in their thinking were still slaves to convention. He cited examples of false patriots, ignorant optimists, worldly clerics, and worthless idols of the public. Even among men who behaved with greater dignity than these, he said bitterly, there were many who were in fact

51. *Zenshū*, 4: 30.
52. *Zenshū*, 4: 23.

contemptible hypocrites. Japan had become a graveyard of the young. There was no freshness of spirit, no originality. What did one see but a docile, mindless acceptance of everything?

Destroy! Yes, destroy! Then perhaps we can begin anew.[53]

Such accounts are hardly sufficient to convince us of the reality of Aoki's authority. Nor does Tōson make plain the effect that these impassioned remarks have on Kishimoto. What bearing do they have on the young man's subsequent conduct? As far as we know, none.

Perhaps the most significant single event in the novel is Aoki's suicide. Yet it fails to move us, simply because Tōson does not explain to our satisfaction the reasons why Aoki should have killed himself. Was it madness, was it disappointment with his own literary career, was it poverty? We have no means of knowing. Shortly after Aoki's death, Suge says to Kishimoto: "It someone were to ask you why Aoki killed himself, you would be hard put to it to find an answer, wouldn't you?" And Kishimoto agrees.[54]

The entire incident, because of the vague, contentless way in which it is treated, seems hardly real to the reader. He presumes that it is significant, since it must indeed have had a great emotional impact on Kishimoto. But Tōson refuses, or is unable, to divulge the details of Kishimoto's reaction to his friend's death. For all the evidence Tōson provides, the death of a distant cousin might have moved Kishimoto as much.

Katsuko also dies—in her case from illness. She has by this time married her fiancé and moved to a distant province. Kishimoto is now once more teaching at the school where he originally met her. He hears of her death from a colleague, the dormitory supervisor, one day at school.

The supervisor, after having talked about various other people, said: "By the way, did you happen to hear about Miss Yasui?" Yasui had been Katsuko's maiden name. "No," said Kishimoto. The other looked at him casually. He seemed to be wondering whether Kishimoto would remember the girl. "Her name was Yasui Katsuko. She used to be a student here, you remember? Well, she died recently." Kishimoto's face went suddenly red. He wanted to ask when and how she had died, but could not bring himself to do so. He had always found it strangely difficult to inquire after Katsuko. On his way home, he thought he saw the ground swell before his eyes; the sky, when he looked at it, would seem suddenly to change its color to bright yellow; and everything around him seemed to be swaying.[55]

Once more, we are left indifferent. Katsuko's existence has never had much reality for us; we can hardly be expected, therefore, to mourn her death with Kishimoto.

The two deaths intensify Kishimoto's sense of purposelessness. And when his elder brother, who is the head of the family, is imprisoned for having unwittingly involved himself in a fraudulent transaction, and he, Kishimoto, is consequently obliged to accept the responsibility of taking care of their mother and the brother's wife, he finds himself in a state of acute depression. He cannot earn enough money to support the family, and he begins to believe himself a complete failure. One day he turns to his mother and asks: "Mother, what did you have in mind when you allowed someone like me to be born?"[56]

With Aoki dead, *Bungakkai* is left leaderless. The magazine is continued by the survivors, but the old enthusiasm gradually dissipates. Kishimoto begins to question his own commitment to literature.

In December of that year, Kishimoto went on a trip to Kazusa, taking with him his sister-in-law who was suffering from beriberi. They sailed by mailboat from Yokohama to Futtsu. Then leaving his sister-in-law behind at a fishing village called Okubo, Kishimoto proceeded to Kominato in Bōshū to see Nichiren's birthplace. In order to get there, he had to go over Mount Kano. The mountain path was full of stones. It followed the top of a valley; and far below, there was a stream. . . . Once he paused along the way and thought he would try his hand at improvised fortunetelling: he would roll some stones down the precipice, and if they fell into the stream, he would continue with his literary activities; if they stopped before they reached it, he would give up writing altogether and get some sort of a job. He watched as the stones rolled down to the bottom. One went right over the stream and landed on the other side; one fell into it; and one stopped halfway down the precipice. He was left just as confused as he had been before.[57]

Soon afterwards, for lack of a better way of earning a living, he finds work as a hand-decorator of chinaware destined for export. He finds the atmosphere in the workshop unbearably depressing and gives up the job at the end of the first day there. Then suddenly and inexplicably, Kishimoto decides there is still hope for him. He will leave Tokyo once more, and try to begin a new life.

55. *Zenshū*, 4: 194.
56. *Zenshū*, 4: 207.
57. *Zenshū*, 4: 199.

Despair led him to a strange decision. He hit upon the idea of going on a journey as a way of escaping his own suffering. And he tried to justify his decision to himself by saying: "My family is of course important. But it is still more important that I find a way of life that is right for me. This is what all of us must do. What is the point of being a good son and brother when one does not even know the purpose of one's own existence?"[58]

A friend finds a post for Kishimoto at a school in Sendai. The novel ends as the train leaves Tokyo, carrying Kishimoto to the distant northeast.

He could hear the melancholy sound of the rain outside. He leaned his head against the window and dreamed hopefully of all that the future might hold for him. He was utterly exhausted. He thought: "I do want to live—even I." The scene outside flashed past his eyes—the grey sky, the trees and grass shining wet, thin mist rising from the rain-soaked ground, hens huddled forlornly under the eaves. Weary of the journey through the rain, most of the other travellers had gone to sleep. The rain, which had been falling steadily, suddenly began to pour down.[59]

The novel, then, is weak because the characters' actions are never based on sufficient motive. Tōson describes but does not explain. This surely is a weakness inherent in the impressionistic technique, which by its very nature cannot be concerned with the examination of the complexities of human behavior. In writing a novel such as *Spring*, therefore, the author must be careful not to enter into the realm where searching questions as to why the characters behave as they do become relevant. *Spring* is a failure not because it is impressionistically written, but because Tōson raises questions in our minds which cannot be answered within the limits he has set for himself. In intention at least, *Spring* is an extended prose lyric. Yet in it Tōson unwittingly allows certain considerations to intrude on our consciousness which would more properly belong in a psychological novel with a well-defined plot.

For all its faults, however, *Spring* is an historically important work. It is an attempt, though not a very successful one, to introduce material of the sort that had never been associated in Japan with the novel before. Whatever else it may be, it is certainly not vulgar entertainment. In trying to write truthfully and lyrically about his own youth, Tōson was bringing to the novel a new kind of emotional commitment. He was bringing to it the truthfulness

58. *Zenshū*, 4: 236.
59. *Zenshū*, 4: 248.

of the poet. And even if he did fail here, he succeeded in his next attempt, where we see his own peculiar conception of realism come to life with some power.

The House

The House was completed in 1911. It is considerably longer than *Spring*, and shows much more careful planning. From the purely technical point of view, it is probably his most successful work: in it, we see a particular technique being applied with more consistency and perhaps more effectiveness than in any of his other novels. "When I wrote *The House*," says Tōson, "I tried to ignore those things which took place outside the house, and to limit myself to scenes inside the house. . . . I wrote in the kitchen, in the front hall, and at night [i.e., in order to describe faithfully the time and place of each scene]. When I wished to describe the sound of the river, I went to the room where it was audible."[60] For the author of *The House*, the details of the backdrop are as important as what the actors do or say. He is equally removed from both: the human voices are hushed and seem to merge with other sounds; and the people move only as distant figures, never intruding on our awareness of the surroundings. None of the characters is allowed to stand out in bold relief. Their thoughts and actions are described accurately but with extreme detachment, just as the details of the surrounding scene are, and they are delved into no further than the latter. Thus there is no personal tragedy in *The House*, but an all-pervading mood of quiet sorrow.

The House is therefore primarily a novel of description, where the author tries to describe accurately only that which his eyes see and his ears hear, and to express his emotions implicitly through detached observations of the surface scene. What Tōson tries to do in *The House* is to keep the interpretive role of the novelist to the absolute minimum and to render the novel as free as possible from an imposed rational construct. The result is what Tōson himself chose to call "impressionism." He once asked: "Does not observing carefully and seriously the incidents of daily life lead the writer naturally to impressionism?"[61] And what he seems to be implying here is that in real life we see the scene around us in a series of separate impressions and that the novelist who imposes on what he has seen a rationalized thread of continuity is merely giving reality an arbitrary and personal interpretation. Here we see how different were Tōson and Sōseki, the two writers who probably have had the greatest influence on the modern Japanese novel.

The novel covers a period of some twelve years beginning in 1898—i.e., from the time Tōson left Sendai to the time immediately preceding the publication of *The House*. However, unlike *Spring* or *A New Life*, the novel concerns Tōson's life only as it relates to his family, and there is hardly a reference in the entire work to himself as an individual personality or to his own private life as a writer. Nor can it be considered a family chronicle in any strict sense. There is no uniformity of pace in the chronological progression, and there is no attempt on Tōson's part to maintain narrative continuity. The time lapse between scenes may be a few years or it may be a few days; and often, a scene will end abruptly in the middle of a conversation, and the next scene may deal with a totally different situation involving different characters. Particular members of the family will claim our attention for a time, then suddenly fade into the background and remain forgotten until they appear again perhaps years later, having as likely as not undergone, during their absence from the scene, crucial experiences which in another kind of novel would have formed the core of the narrative.

In the scheme of the novel, neither the incidents nor the persons have much significance in themselves. They have proportionately no more content, say, than distant sounds and figures described in a lyrical poem about a lonely autumnal scene. If they are more detailed and possess more concrete reality, it is because *The House* is a novel—and a long one at that—and not a lyrical poem. *The House* is nevertheless a poet's novel. It abounds in scenes which are clearly rich in dramatic potential, yet nowhere does Tōson depart from his set purpose: the lyricist always remains in control, and the dramatist is never allowed to assert himself. For this reason, *The House* at times may seem to the reader far too uneventful, much too lacking in drama; but it is for this reason too that it is one of the best executed of modern Japanese novels.

On one level, the novel is about two houses: the one that the author springs from, which he calls Koizumi, and the one that his elder sister has married into, which he calls Hashimoto. On another level, it concerns the individual members of the two houses. The chief of these are: Koizumi Sankichi (Tōson) and his wife Oyuki; Hashimoto Tatsuo and his wife Otane, who is Sankichi's elder sister; their son Shōta; and Koizumi Minoru, Sankichi's elder brother and head of the Koizumi house.

Both the Koizumis and the Hashimotos have been families of some prominence in Kiso, the mountainous area behind Nagoya. The Koizumi family, though not samurai, is over three hundred years old, and can trace back their ancestry directly to the original founder of the village. Right up to the Restoration and for some years after, their role has been approximately that of the village squire. But by the time the novel begins, the head of the family, Minoru, has moved to Tokyo. Their large house in Kiso has been destroyed by fire, their property has gone; and without the duties an heir to the Koizumi house would have inherited before the Restoration, Minoru has no ties left with his ancestral home. He has now been living in Tokyo for some years with his wife and daughters, engaged in business. He has not been successful. Indeed, he has recently come out of jail, where he was sent for having become involved—innocently, we gather—in a shady transaction. He will go to jail again for a similar offence. He is, in other words, a stock Japanese figure of post-Restoration days: the man of gentle background who simply does not know how to handle himself in the modern business world.

The Hashimotos have a somewhat different origin. They were samurai before the Restoration. Now they sell medicines which they make up at home from prescriptions handed down to them as family secrets. Theirs is considered a gentle occupation, however, and they still count themselves among the small class of gentry that live in the town of Kiso Fukushima. At the beginning of the book, we find them in comfortable circumstances, with a half dozen people in their employ. But it becomes apparent later that Tatsuo, the head of the family, is not unlike Minoru when it comes to money matters: in time he too allows himself to be associated with a speculative venture that proves ruinous.

Neither of the two is avaricious or dishonest. They are simply misfits whose fathers did not teach them the rules of survival under modern conditions. They have no understanding of money, yet cannot desist from playing at being financiers. All the social institutions that had once guaranteed them their place in society have gone, but their family pride and self-esteem have remained intact, and they try in vain to retain or to win back for themselves a way of life which they think is rightfully theirs. By temperament and upbringing they are fit only for the protected life of small gentry. Under their inept leadership the two houses are eventually reduced to bankruptcy.

Having come out of prison, Minoru now lives modestly with his wife and two daughters. He still imagines that he is a businessman and is hopeful that he will reestablish himself.

> He said that he had learned a lesson from his previous mistakes and made it a rule to wear only cotton clothes. There were many things he had to do. The land on which their large house in the country had stood, the woods and the fields that had belonged to the family—these were now in other people's hands. He must somehow get them back. He owed that to his ancestors. Besides, it was for him a matter of personal honor, of self-esteem. And then there were all those debts that had to be settled.[62]

No one in the family seems to know the exact nature or the extent of his business commitments. All they know is that he is backing the manufacture and eventual marketing of some kind of new vehicle. They hope rather forlornly that this time, Minoru will succeed. But again he fails. He has incurred impossibly heavy debts while floating the scheme, and once more goes to jail. Morihiko, the second of the Koizumi brothers, and Sankichi, the fourth and youngest, must now support Minoru's wife and daughters and Sōzō, the third brother, who is dying of a venereal disease contracted in his youth and who has so far been taken care of by Minoru.

Some years pass. Oshun, Minoru's elder daughter, is now of college age. Sankichi's wife, Oyuki, has gone to Hokkaido to spend the summer with her family, and he is left alone in the house. He arranges for Oshun and Morihiko's daughter, Onobu, to come and live with him to help him keep house during

Oyuki's absence. Oshun arrives, accompanied by her younger sister Otsuru, who has just come for the day. Their cousin Onobu is already there. In characteristic fashion, Tōson very casually informs the reader of Minoru's return from his long second imprisonment and suggests with delicacy the pathos of his situation.

The door opened, and Oshun came into the house with her younger sister. Onobu welcomed them happily. Hearing their voices, Sankichi appeared from the back of the house.

"Hullo, uncle," said Oshun. "I would have come sooner, but I've had an awful lot of studying to do." Then turning to Onobu, she said: "It must have been hard work for you, all alone."

Onobu said, "I'm so glad Otsuru was able to come too."

"Her school is having a holiday today, so I brought her along."

"Hasn't the term ended yet where she is?" asked Sankichi.

"Their summer holidays start very late," said Oshun. "By the way, father sends his best wishes."

"I'm so glad you've come," said Onobu again.

Minoru had only recently come home after his long absence. While he was away, his two daughters had been kept alive by their mother's makeshift efforts and by whatever help their uncles had been able to provide. Sankichi remembered that Oshun had just finished primary school when he was first married. Now, she was old enough to come like this and look after him. It was many years since she had last spent her summer holidays with him.

"Otsuru," said Oshun, "why don't you go and play in the garden?"

"How she has grown," said Sankichi.

"Hasn't she? Look at her dress, it's become much too short for her."

Otsuru grinned sheepishly and went down to the garden.

"Oshun, what's your father doing these days?"

"Nothing in particular yet. But you know, he gets up terribly early in the mornings. He says we've had a hard time because of him, and he's going to make up for it by doing the housework. He gets up when it's still dark and starts cooking breakfast. He says he got used to getting up early while he was away and couldn't sleep late now even if he wanted to. By the time mother gets up, breakfast is all ready."

"How sad—"

"When it was only the three of us, the house used to get rather untidy sometimes. But with father around, we don't have to worry any more. It's all rather strange, don't you think?"

There was a squeal from the garden. Otsuru had slipped and fallen down. Onobu rushed out. Oshun laughed, and followed her cousin. Together the two brushed the dirt off little Otsuru's clothes.[63]

A few days later, Minoru himself pays Sankichi a visit.

63. *Zenshū*, 5: 237–38.

They went into Sankichi's room and sat down. The girls were out. Sankichi went to the brazier and made some tea. He came back with a cup for his elder brother.

After his mistakes, Minoru had conscientiously kept away from his younger brothers. He had not yet seen Morihiko since his return. He had seen Sankichi only once before this.

"Where is Oshun?" he asked.

"She went out with Onobu to do some shopping in Shinjuku."

"Is she any good at housekeeping?"

"Oh yes. They've both been very helpful. As a matter of fact, I told them to go and buy themselves a summer dress each today."

"They must be very excited." Minoru then made a reference to Sankichi's children who had died not long before from illness. He continued: "But you know, I've decided it's a mistake to brood too much over one's misfortunes. Not to care—that's the only way. Not to care about what happens to one's wife, to one's children, or, for that matter, to oneself."

He was like a pedestrian on a busy street, trying to weave his way as carefully as possible through the crowd. He was not going to get himself emotionally involved with his brothers, if he could help it. He made no attempt to talk to Sankichi about his own recent bitter experience; nor did he try to apologize for all the trouble he had caused. His manner was that of the head of an ancient house, talking to a dependent.

His own lack of money seemed to hurt his pride more than anything else. Their sick brother, Sōzō, who was by rights Minoru's responsibility, was now living with strangers, and Sankichi was paying for his support. There had been many other expenses besides, which Minoru had left to Sankichi to settle. He was now about to command his younger brother to make another contribution.

"I just borrowed forty yen from N," he said. "I told him that he could get it back from you. You must find the money somehow."

Sankichi began to object, but he was quickly interrupted by Minoru, who brought out a piece of paper and, showing it to him, said: "Here, look at this. It's a list of various things in the house. They are yours now. Just tell yourself you bought them for forty yen." On the list neatly written out in a small hand, were a chest of drawers, a carpet, a table, a cigarette box, drinking ware, and so on.

"I'll leave it to you, then, to take care of the debt," Minoru said, and left hurriedly.

Surely, Sankichi thought, he could at least have thanked me for looking after his family during his absence. But he also knew that it was impossible for his brother to do so.

Oshun and Onobo returned, carrying parcels under their arms. They had bought their dresses.[64]

Though Minoru seems less inclined now to take risks, neither Morihiko nor Sankichi can feel confident that their brother will handle his affairs any more capably than he has done in the past. Minoru himself has tentatively mentioned the possibility of his going to Manchuria to start a new career, and his brothers decide that it is time he was made to go.

They were not concerned merely for their brother's welfare. They had been hurt too often by his failures, and were now intent on protecting themselves. And so on the last day of the rainy season, Sankichi set out for Minoru's house.

He found himself on a street where the air was so heavy and humid that he felt he was in a swamp. Life around him seemed depressed. The ditches on both sides of him were full and deep, and there was mud everywhere. The next street he came to seemed more removed and quiet. There was a row of houses, all with outside gates. In one of them lived Minoru and his family.

He heard Oshun saying, "Uncle Sankichi is here." She came out to the front hall. She had obviously been waiting for him. Then Onobu appeared. [Oshun is now back with her family, and Onobu, Morihiko's daughter, is temporarily staying with them.]

"Is your uncle Morihiko here?" Sankichi asked Oshun.

"Yes. He's been waiting for you."

She looked worried. She had probably guessed why her uncles were there.

"Otsuru," she said to her little sister uneasily, "go out and play with your friends."

"Now, that's a very good idea," said Okura, their mother. Then Oshun looked hard at her cousin, as if to say: "Do use some imagination, Onobu, and don't stay around at a time like this." But Onobu seemed not to know what to do. She had only recently moved there from Sankichi's house. She remained where she was, looking very nervous.

While waiting for Sankichi, Minoru had tidied the room and got the tea ready. The three brothers now sat down to drink the tea before beginning their business. Minoru stood up and, going to the cupboard, brought out an old wooden box. He dusted it and handed it to Sankichi. "I'll leave this with you," he said. His tone was grave. It was as though he was appointing Sankichi to some sort of official custodianship. The box contained a document in their father's handwriting. There had been other mementos of their father, but they had gradually disappeared, and now this old box was all that remained.

Morihiko said, "Let's get down to business, shall we?"

Oshun was filled with apprehension. She looked at her mother, who sat by the door, trying to hear what the men in the next room were saying; and at her cousin, who sat silently, head bowed, by the brazier. She stood up and went into the next room. She sat down by her desk in the corner. She listened carefully, so that she could remember later everything that had been said.

"That kind of weak talk won't do," Morihiko was saying; "if you want to go to Manchuria, then go."

"You're quite right, of course," Minoru said. "I feel quite fit, and if I could be sure that all my affairs would be taken care of after I'd left, I'd go tomorrow."

"No need to worry about that. There's me, and there's Sankichi—"

"It's good of you to say so. So long as I can count on you two, I'll go happily."

Oshun was shocked. Were men always this callous? She looked at her father. He was showing his account book, filled with small figures, to her uncles. Then Morihiko began suddenly to give vent to all the resentment he had been harboring towards his brother for so many years. Oshun noticed that he did not address her father as "elder brother." Instead, he kept calling him "you." With voice lowered but angrily, he attacked her father at length for all his past misconduct. The latter's face had gone pale.

Oshun wondered how much further her uncle would go. In his usual way, he was being extreme. Her resilient father sat and listened, saying nothing. She had at first been inclined to blame him; but now, she felt only pity.

She was much relieved to hear her father say: "Oshun, you can serve the lunch now." She helped her mother carry the food into the inner room.

Minoru once more became the head of the house. "There isn't much," he said, "but please start."

The three brothers began to eat. Though no one said so, it was a farewell occasion. Now that he was seated at the table, Morihiko could not but change his manner.

"This is delicious, I must say," he said, praising the soup. He seemed relaxed as he ate.

"Do have more," said Okura. Her manner reminded the company of the days when the Koizumi house had been more prosperous.

The lunch ended cheerfully.

Morihiko and Sankichi came out of their brother's house. After they had walked through the mud for half a block or so, Morihiko turned to Sankichi and said jocularly: "Well, my words had some effect on our dear old brother, wouldn't you say?" But it was no use. They were in no mood even for wry humor. Once more, they were going to have to look after Minoru's family and their brother Sōzō.

After her uncles had gone, Oshun went out in search of her sister. She had to find her quickly; after all, she thought with a shiver, their father was leaving for Manchuria the next day. At the first house she went to, she was told that Otsuru had indeed been playing there but had just left. Quickly she walked home.

She had never thought that her father would go to Manchuria so soon. He was busily packing, and seemed cheerful. He refused to say much about his forthcoming trip. She watched him as he bustled about. She then looked at her mother, who was simply bewildered; and at her sister, who was too young to be deeply affected; and she could not help crying.

It seemed to her only yesterday that after the long, painful period of waiting she had at last been able to see her father again. And now, they were to be separated once more. No one was to blame but her uncles. Were they not driving him away from his helpless family? She could hardly bear the bitterness that filled her little heart. She began to hate all her relations, to whom she, her mother, and her sister would now have to go for help. She cried, not only because she felt personally humiliated, but because she mourned the decline of her family.

But she was not going to let her uncles bully them. She must try to be strong. What was the good of crying? She had her weak, aging mother to think of. That night, she stayed up late with her mother and helped her unfortunate father get everything ready for the journey. "Mother," she said, "I don't suppose we'll sleep much, but let us go to bed."

Minoru got up before dawn. He was followed by Okura and Oshun. "Listen, mother, we can hear the cock crowing," Oshun said, as she dressed. The electric bulb hanging from the ceiling cast a forlorn, reddish light. Okura started the fire in the kitchen, then brought in the embers on a small shovel and put them in the brazier. By this time, Onobu and Otsuru were up.

Since Minoru's father's time, the Koizumis had ceased observing Buddhist rites. So in Minoru's house there was only the small Shinto shrine. He now went to it to offer his prayers. He felt that his father was there, come to bless his son. He clapped his hands and bid farewell to his ancestors.

Okura and Oshun had laid out the breakfast for him by the brazier. They were weeping quietly. Minoru called the family to the table and asked them to drink their farewell cups of tea with him.

The cock crew again. The night was coming to an end at last.

He would not let the family come outside to see him off. "You must stay inside," he said, and went out of the gate alone. He had his courage and his strong constitution. But he was over fifty. In his pocket, he had just enough money to take him to Kobe, where his brother-in-law, Tatsuo, was living. The Manchurian plains were far away. In all likelihood, he thought, he would never be able to come home. Bravely, he walked away from the house where his wife and daughters would now live without him.[65]

Unlike Minoru, Hashimoto Tatsuo first appears in the book as a prosperous, busy, and even responsible man. He has two grown children: Osen, a charming and mentally deficient girl, who, because of her defect, will never marry; Shōta, an intelligent and frustrated young man who does not relish the prospect of succeeding to his family business and being a country gentleman all his life. We see Tatsuo as an affectionate and kindly man. He is obviously fond of his children and of his wife, Otane, who is Sankichi's elder sister. And except for his slight anxiety about Shōta, he seems generally contented.

Sankichi, who is spending the summer at their large house in Kiso Fukushima as the novel opens, is particularly impressed by Tatsuo's energetic management of the family business. From eight in the morning until sundown Tatsuo is busily occupied, in a supervisory capacity, with bookkeeping, preparation of medicines, ordering, and selling. "But this was not all," Tōson adds.

> As one of the local gentry, he was obliged to make himself available for consultation on all kinds of problems, and often he had to take an active part in local affairs. He tried to avoid politics, however, and he spent as much time as he could managing his family business. His industriousness was such that it amazed Sankichi.[66]

Yet Otane is not entirely at ease. Tatsuo has not always been a model husband—woman-chasing, she believes, is a hereditary disease of the Hashimoto men—and she is afraid that his present conscientious behavior may be only temporary. She thinks, and quite rightly, that she can sense a certain restlessness in her husband. But what she does not realize is that Tatsuo's problem is not another woman in his life, but the fact that he has been spending far more money than he can afford. He, it seems, is rather conscious of the prestige of his house and is fearful of being accused of meanness unbecoming to the head of a prominent local family. Otane on her part is equally unrealistic about money. She is a gentlewoman; she therefore must not and will not concern herself with money matters. When, some time after Sankichi's visit, the family is on the verge of bankruptcy, she has only a vague premonition of the coming disaster.

Tatsuo, without Otane's or Shōta's knowledge, has for some years been investing his capital unsoundly in an effort to increase his income. He fails completely. He will soon be declared bankrupt. Rather than stay and face the disgrace, he decides to flee from Kiso Fukushima. (Tōson hints in the passage quoted below that he has not been above embezzlement.) He suggests to his unsuspecting wife that she go to Itō, the resort in Izu, for a rest. He will take her there, he tells her, but he cannot stay with her: he must proceed to Tokyo to attend to some business matters. For some reason—she herself does not know exactly why—she is reluctant to leave the house. But finally she agrees to go.

> They changed trains at Akabane. By the time they got on the Tōkaido train, it was near sunset. Tatsuo lay down along the seat. Otane put the rug over her husband and sat listening to the sound of the train. Restlessly, Tatsuo sat up again. On his dignified, well-bred face there was somehow a look of pain. There was fear in his eyes, as though he was being chased by something he could not quite see.

"Is anything the matter?" asked Otane worriedly. "If you can spare the time, why don't you stay in Itō with me and rest?"

"I don't have that kind of time," Tatsuo said. "As soon as my business is finished in Tokyo, I have to rush back home. I don't have a minute to spare."

Tatsuo was the kind of man who could not rest content with merely the management of the family business. He held an important post in the bank at home. The day was approaching when the books were to be examined.

To relieve the monotony of the journey, Otane brought out the fruit that she had bought at one of the stations and offered a piece to her husband. He began to peel it with his pocket knife. His hands were strangely unsteady, and he nicked a finger.

"There really is something the matter with me," Tatsuo said and tried to appear amused. Otane, nonplussed, looked at her husband. She had never seen him behave quite so oddly.

They made the long journey in one lap. They were exhausted when they arrived at their hotel in Kōzu late that night.

These two, used to living among the mountains of Kiso, were kept awake by the sound of the waves. The next morning they had breakfast together in their room. They could see the sea from where they sat.

Otane was concerned lest she was taking up too much of her husband's time. "If you're busy," she said, "don't come with me any further. All I have to do now is get on the ship, and so long as the weather holds, I'll be in Itō in no time at all. Really, I can go by myself."

"Well, if you say so, perhaps I should leave you here. But are you sure you'll be all right?"

"Of course. I can manage perfectly well by myself. After all, this isn't my first trip to Itō. Besides, I'm sure there'll be plenty of people I know there."

"All right then. I really am terribly busy. There's some business concerning the bank that I have to take care of in Tokyo. And then there are a lot of other things too."

The maid came in to tell them when the ship would be sailing. They noticed that some of the guests were leaving for the railway station. It seemed that there was a train about to leave for Tokyo.

She said to her husband: "Why don't you go on this train?"

"Don't fuss. Just think of the time I'm saving by not going to Itō. There are plenty of other trains."

"But you said yourself you hadn't a minute to spare. I just thought you would want to leave at once."

"No, no. I'll see you off, at least."

Otane could not understand it. Her husband sat there, smoking restlessly. Obviously, he could not relax; yet he looked as though he did not have the strength to move.

They heard the whistle of the train. Tatsuo took no notice. He continued to gaze at the sea.

It was time for her to go. The two left the inn, and went down the path, shaded by the ancient pines, towards the harbor. They walked over the fine sand and came to where the incoming tide washed over the pebbles. The other passengers were already there. The small boat that was to take them to the ship was moored just off shore, and the boatman had to carry each passenger to it. Finally it was Otane's turn. She said goodbye to her husband and got on the sturdy back of the boatman. The water foamed as the man waded roughly through the waves.

The boat rolled gently on towards the ship. Otane watched her husband's lonely figure on the shore. Very soon, it became impossible for her to see his face clearly. That she was travelling alone did not worry her in the least. She had made the same trip a number of times before. Besides, the weather was fine. But she was uneasy about her husband. And on the ship, she began to feel very forlorn. He was not with her any more.[67]

Otane is not permitted to leave Itō for almost a year. The rest of the family, in particular her son Shōta and her brother Morihiko, have decided not to break the bad news to her at once and to keep her away from home until affairs have been settled. They send her expense money and "advise" her to stay in Izu and make the most of her holiday.

She is kept in the dark for some months; then, when she has come to suspect the worst, they tell her that Tatsuo has absconded, leaving the Hashimoto house in a state of bankruptcy. Some more months pass before she receives word that she may now leave Izu. She must go to Tokyo, however, and not to her home in Kiso.

It was now early June. The long-awaited day came at last. With no one helping her, Otane hurriedly prepared for her journey to Tokyo. All this time, she had not heard one word from her husband. But she could not stop thinking about him.

She said goodbye to the people she had come to know well during her stay. The woman that now sailed away from the Izu coast was an entirely different person from the woman that had come there. The coastline that she had seen from the ship, the ports they had stopped at to pick up cargo—these she saw once more; and the sorrow she had felt a year before at parting from her husband now returned.

The ship arrived in Kōzu. The passengers quickly got on the little boat that had come to take them to the shore. A large wave came and heaved the boat up high, then seemed to carry it all the way. In a little while, Otane was standing again on the very spot where her husband's lonely figure had stood as she sailed away.

The bright June sun shone on the Sea of Sagami. Otane could scarcely pull herself away from the shore. She walked over the same hot sand and up the same path under the pines. She reached the top of the small hill overlooking the beach and stopped at the inn for lunch. "Well, well, madame," said the inn-keeper innocently, "you have had a long vacation, I must say." And with professional courtesy he answered Otane's polite inquiries.[68]

She stays in Tokyo for a while, then goes to live with Sankichi, who is now teaching in a town not many miles distant from her home. Finally, after an absence of a year and a half, she is allowed to return to Kiso Fukushima. There she begins to live a much altered life. Towards the end of the novel, Sankichi again visits the Hashimoto home. Twelve years have passed since his last visit there, and all the happiness and prosperity he saw then is now gone. Tatsuo, after living more or less in hiding in Nagoya and then in Kobe, has gone to Manchuria. Shōta is in Nagoya, trying unsuccessfully to make good in business. With neither of the men at home to look after the family business, the Hashimotos have had to adopt formally a young man by the name of Kōsaku, who was once a boy apprentice of theirs. He is now the master. He runs the reduced establishment with a firmness and economy unknown in Tatsuo's time, which fact Otane regards with distaste. She feels—somewhat ungratefully, but understandably—that no gentleman would ever have been such a hard taskmaster and so economy-minded. She will have little to do with Kōsaku or his wife, both of whom she treats as interlopers though they are technically members of the family. Lonely and embittered, and pining for her husband, she leads a secluded existence in the empty-seeming large house. Her only daily solace is the companionship of her retarded and now unhappy daughter Osen, and Shōta's wife, Toyose, who is impatient to leave the gloomy country house and join her husband in Nagoya.

The morning after his arrival, Sankichi goes outside to have a look at the grounds. He finds Otane sweeping around the ornamental stones in a corner of the inner garden. She leads him up some stone steps to a spot which once overlooked their outbuildings and orchard. These have disappeared, and there is now a naked ravine. Smiling sadly, Otane points her broom at the laborers below busily constructing a railway line. As they walk back to the house, Sankichi notices the fear in Otane's eyes.

Later, when they are seated in one of the large and rather bare inner rooms, Sankichi says encouragingly to his sister:

68. *Zenshū*, 5: 166–67.

"But all things considered, you seem to have managed to keep quite a few things around the house."

"Yes, thanks to everybody's efforts," Otane said. Then she added: "But you know, when I first came home after staying with you, I could hardly bear to look at what they had done to our house. It was a shock, I can tell you."

"By the way, I hear that Tatsuo-san has gone to Manchuria."

"Yes, that's right."

"I suppose you can't help feeling you've been deserted."

"Well, while he was in Kobe, I still had the feeling he would come back to me sooner or later. But when I heard that he had gone to Manchuria, I thought to myself, 'this is the end.' "

"It can't be helped. Just try to forget him."

"It's easier said than done," she said, with a crooked smile. "How can I ever forget him?"

A harsh sound reached them from the outside. It was one of those trucks, laden with stones, running on the track at the bottom of the ravine. Grimly, as if in pain, Otane waited until the sound died away. Then she began to talk worriedly about her son, Shōta. She said, more than once: "I do hope things work out well for him."[69]

Shōta is only three years younger than Sankichi, and they are more like brothers than uncle and nephew. Indeed, Sankichi feels a closer bond with Shōta than he does with any of his three elder brothers. As for Shōta, he is a frustrated young man who is not sure what he wants, and he finds in Sankichi the kind of sympathy and understanding he cannot find in anyone else. He is intelligent, but like his father, proud and erratic and quite unsuited to business. He is hardly the man to set aright the family finances after his father's sudden departure.

Rather than stay at home and manage the family business, he goes to Tokyo to seek his fortune. Tōson writes:

For a while he tried living in a small rented house in Tokyo with Toyose, but he soon gave that up. He sent his wife back to Kiso and began to wander here and there in search of a job. It was not in his nature to rest content with some ordinary means of earning a living. With little more than the fare in his pocket, he went to distant Hokkaido and then to Korsakov in Sakhalin. After having failed there, he returned to Aomori, where he lived abjectly for a time in some cheap hotel. Of course he had no capital, so that his venture had little chance of success. Once he thought he would try speculating in Iwaki coal. And once he decided to go to South China and went so far as to take conversation lessons. Everything had ended abortively. He was still looking for something he could do. He grew more and more anxious.[70]

69. *Zenshū*, 5: 403–4.
70. *Zenshū*, 5: 210.

Eventually he finds employment with a firm of stockjobbers. It is not a very respectable occupation, but it appeals to his flamboyant nature. There is a daredevil, big-city stylishness about it; besides, it offers opportunities for quick profit. Before long he wins the confidence of his employers and is given a position of trust. He begins to earn a fairly sizable income. Yet he cannot be contented. There is no real security in stockjobbing; moreover, he is a little too well bred and sensitive to remain impervious to the loud vulgarity of his daily surroundings and the desperate profit-seeking of his colleagues. Craving the company of someone who lives outside of this mercenary world and who will understand his sense of aimlessness and disappointment, he continually visits Sankichi. (The latter has by this time returned to Tokyo after some years of schoolmastering in the provinces, and has become a novelist by profession.)

One evening, Shōta drops in on Sankichi and Oyuki with his customary informality. Sankichi has been out and has just returned home and taken off his city clothes.

Shōta gossiped lightly about the theatre and such matters for a while, then said: "Uncle, I haven't eaten yet." Couldn't they go to some restaurant, he wondered, and while away this pleasant early winter evening together?

Sankichi turned to his wife and said: "Oyuki, get my clothes out again, will you? Shōta says he's about to go out somewhere for a meal, so I'll go with him."

Oyuki said, laughing: "How happy-go-lucky men are." Sankichi put on the European-style suit that he had taken off only a few minutes before. Shōta was dressed rather dashingly in Japanese clothes. Together they walked out of the house.

"You really are beginning to look like a city broker," Sankichi said. "And where are you taking me?"

"Leave everything to me, uncle. Tonight, for a change, I'm going to be the host."

Shōta had of late become more and more drawn to the bright gaiety of night life. The tumult and the confusion of life at the exchange—the excited buying and selling that followed a sudden drop or rise in shares, the abrupt changes in men's fortunes, the crazed look in the eyes, the wild cursing—so affected him that he could not relax any more. It had become impossible for him to spend an evening quietly at home. Like insects that must fly towards the light at night, he was drawn to those places where he would be near other people. They went part of the way by streetcar; the rest they went by rickshaw. The rickshaws sped over a large bridge first, then a small bridge.[71]

Shōta's affluence is short-lived. The firm he is associated with goes bankrupt, and he is left without employment. For months he searches in vain for another job in Tokyo. Finally he hears of an opening in Nagoya and decides he has no choice but to leave the capital. In Nagoya he dabbles in speculation on his own and fails completely. Later, when Sankichi goes to Nagoya after his visit to Otane, he finds Shōta and Toyose (the latter has in the meantime left her mother-in-law and joined her husband) living in gloomy rented rooms. Shōta tells Sankichi that his chest has been giving him trouble. In fact, he says, he has coughed up blood twice since his coming to Nagoya. But, he adds with pathetic optimism, the doctor has assured him that with proper care he should last at least ten more years.

It was evening, and Sankichi had to catch the night train to Tokyo. Shōta wanted to see his uncle off. The two went to the station by streetcar. They arrived some minutes before the train was due to leave. Shōta quietly paced up and down the platform. The lights were just coming on. He stopped, as though a thought had suddenly struck him, and said: "Both aunt Oyuki and my wife are in their prime, wouldn't you say?" He seemed to find the thought unbearably oppressive.

Sankichi got onto the train. Shōta stood by the window, holding his platform ticket. Everything about him—the look in his eyes, the way he stood—suggested sharp pain and disappointment. The conductor rushed past, blowing his whistle. Shōta brought his face close to the window and peered in. He seemed to want to have a good look at his uncle. Sankichi too stood helplessly by the window like a rain-sodden hen.

"Remember me to aunt Oyuki," Shōta said, and the train began to move. The station lights and vague outlines of people standing on the platform flashed past. Sankichi imagined Shōta walking back to his lodgings. He remembered how he had advised Shōta to go home to Kiso for a rest and how the latter had shaken his head and said that he wanted to go on trying. Sankichi then thought of Otane in Kiso, who knew nothing of her son's illness or his recent failures, and who put all her hopes in him.

"Poor fellow," Sankichi thought. For a long time he remained standing by the window.[72]

Some months after his return to Tokyo, Sankichi hears that Shōta has gone into a hospital. Then one day he receives a telegram from Shōta asking him to come and see him. Sankichi leaves for Nagoya immediately. Shōta knows he is dying, and he simply wants to see his uncle again.

72. Zenshū, 5: 421–22.

Sankichi could not remain in Nagoya long. He stayed with the others at Shōta's bedside until the afternoon. Since it did not seem that Shōta would die immediately, he decided to leave. He formally asked those in the room to take good care of his nephew.

The time came for him to say goodbye. He stood close to the bed, and put out his hand, clammy from the heat. "Shōta-san," he said, "I shall have to leave."

Some time passed. Then, as Sankichi made to go, Shōta desperately held on to the other's hand, grasping it as firmly as he could. He said: "I am not going to give up. I must see you again." The tears he had been holding back suddenly began to flow down his cheeks.

"Of course, of course," said Otane, who was sitting by her son, and covered her face. In the next room sat Kōsaku, the successor to the family business, with his head bowed.

A wash basin for visitors stood at the end of the corridor. There Sankichi carefully washed his hands, then went back to say goodbye to his sister. Shōta's wife, Toyose, was not in the room. Through the open door, Shōta watched his uncle walk away. Sankichi was accompanied by Kōsaku as far as the hospital gate. When he was outside and alone, he began to weep violently.[73]

A week later, Sankichi receives news of Shōta's death.

Sankichi's role in relation to the main theme of *The House* is more removed and, at the same time, more complex than that of the others. He is both observer and participant, but the former role predominates. The novel is for the most part written from his point of view, and it is his almost continuous presence that enables the author to maintain with some consistency the desired perspective.[74]

As one of the actors Sankichi is involved in the ruin of the two old houses but not, of course, to the same degree as are Minoru, Tatsuo, Otane, or Shōta. On one occasion he says to his brother Morihiko: "Wherever we go, whatever we do, we seem never to be able to escape from our sense of obligation to our ancient houses. Why don't we simply rid ourselves of this burden once and for all?"[75] Elsewhere he tells Shōta that they should all forget about continuing the old family line and decide to begin their own lives anew. As far as he is concerned, the Koizumi house has come to an end.[76] He is a younger son, he has his own life

73. *Zenshū*, 5: 438–39.
74. There are passages in the novel where the author departs from Sankichi's point of view, such as the descriptions of Otane's sojourn in Izu and Minoru's departure for Manchuria, but these are very few.
75. *Zenshū*, 5: 381.
76. *Zenshū*, 5: 324.

to live, and he must not allow himself and his own immediate family to lose their independent identity. Thus side by side with the main theme which concerns the two houses and the characters in relation to them, there is a subordinate theme running through the novel which concerns only Sankichi and Oyuki in their capacity as husband and wife.

For two years since his return from Sendai, Sankichi has been living with his brother Morihiko and his family in Tokyo. He decides that he would like to live in the provinces again; and when the headmaster of a school in a small town in Kiso offers him a post, he accepts without much hesitation. There, in peaceful rural surroundings, he hopes to begin a more settled and responsible kind of life. His family have for some time been urging him to get married. He is now inclined to be persuaded. He has lived the life of a homeless wanderer for too long; marriage is perhaps what he needs. So when he is presented with a suitable candidate—a daughter of a successful merchant in Hokkaido and a graduate of the girls' college where he used to teach—he allows his family to proceed with the negotiations. The parties quickly come to an agreement. The marriage ceremony takes place in Tokyo; immediately after, Sankichi leaves for Kiso with Oyuki, his bride, to start a home of his own. *The House*, then, begins with the decline of two old houses and the establishing of a new.

Sankichi has already been to the country town and rented a house. It is old and shabby but large, and is situated in a quiet neighborhood. It used to be a samurai residence, Sankichi tells Oyuki. To Oyuki, who is used to the comforts of upper middle-class life, the prospect of living as the mistress of this gaunt house (with the aid, moreover, of only a student houseboy) in a cheerless and remote country town seems rather bleak. But she is a bride, about to embark on a novel experience. She accepts her condition uncomplainingly and with cheerful determination. As for Sankichi, he feels a kind of contentment he has never known before. For a while, at any rate, their married life is happy enough —perhaps even idyllic.

There is a field at the back of their house, and Sankichi, whose contentment has put him in a bucolic frame of mind, decides to try his hand at kitchen gardening.

Again the next day Sankichi went out into the field as soon as he returned from school.

After he had begun working, Oyuki appeared. She had come along the path between the mulberry trees and the fence. She was followed by the student who was living with them.

"Just don't stand there watching," said Sankichi. "Try helping a little."

"But we did come to help," said Oyuki, laughing.

"In that case, you two can start taking those stones away." Sankichi then added: "You know, one really has to be trained from childhood for this kind of work. At this rate, it doesn't look as if I'll ever become a farmer."

Cheerfully he started digging again. There seemed to be no end to the stones.

Oyuki covered her hair with a cloth, then tucked up the skirts of her kimono, and together with the student began to work. Their job was to take the stones away in a basket and dump them by the stream. After that, they had to take away the weeds which Sankichi had dug up and left at the edge of the field. Mud still stuck to the tough roots, and Oyuki found them terribly heavy. The three worked hard in the sun.

In true peasant fashion Sankichi had tied a hand towel around his head. "Now, that looks quite authentic," teased Oyuki. "But I am not sure about the spectacles." The student stood by, looking amused. Sankichi smiled wryly and wiped the sweat off his face with his dirty hands.[77]

But their happiness does not last long. Oyuki can find no relief from her daily routine of housework. Not only is she the wife of a poor country schoolmaster, but the town they live in can hardly offer her the kind of social life she craves. The incongruously fashionable clothes she brought with her now lie unused in the closet. Perhaps from boredom or from loneliness, she begins to exchange letters with an old sweetheart who is one of her father's more promising employees. One day, she carelessly leaves a letter that she has written to the young man lying on a chest of drawers. It catches Sankichi's eye. He has by this time become suspiciously aware of the letters that continue to come for his wife from Hokkaido. Oyuki has gone out and, finding the temptation irresistible, he opens her letter and reads it. The young man's name is Tsutomu, and he is about to marry one of Oyuki's sisters. The content of the letter is not particularly incriminating: she has been very busy, Oyuki writes, and is sorry that she has not written for so long; she is happy that Tsutomu has decided to marry her sister. What really hurts Sankichi, however, is the way his wife signs off the letter: "To

my very dear Tsutomu, from Oyuki without hope."⁷⁸ Sankichi
loses all sense of propriety. He must see what Tsutomu has been
writing to Oyuki. He searches furiously all over the house for his
rival's letters; finally he finds a torn fragment of a letter buried
among waste-paper stuffed into an empty coal sack. On it are
written passionate expressions of love for Oyuki.

For two days he says nothing to his wife about his discovery.
Then he writes an extremely emotional letter to Tsutomu, in
which he sympathizes with the young merchant's unhappiness
and asks that his own predicament be understood. Could they not
all forget the past and establish a new, happier relationship? The
letter is embarrassingly generous. When he has finished writing,
he calls Oyuki to his side and reads the letter. She is speechless
with shame and, one supposes, remorse. (Tōson does not tell us
what Oyuki's real feelings are.) Sankichi tries to be reasonable
and forgiving, but he is not altogether successful.

"What is past is past"—that was what Oyuki wanted her husband's attitude
to be. But he could not quite bring himself to feel that way.
Sankichi was overcome with loneliness. And because he could not stand his
loneliness, he tried to prove to his wife that he could be as gentle to her as any
man. He went out of his way to be considerate that day. But all the while he
felt a bitter pain.⁷⁹

The incident brings to their marriage an undercurrent of bitterness and coldness that even the birth of a baby daughter some
months later cannot dispel.

The house somehow came to seem empty. There were times now when the
two would sit down to a meal in silence, not looking at each other.
It hurt Oyuki to see her husband so silent and hard. And now there were so
many times when she simply did not know what this difficult husband of hers
would say next. One minute he would look at Ofusa, their little daughter, and
say lovingly: "She has cheeks just like my mother's." Then the next minute an
exchange such as this would ensue: "Are you sure Ofusa is my child?"
"Don't be silly. Whose child can she be if she isn't yours?" There was
nothing that hurt Oyuki more than this kind of senseless talk.
Or he would suddenly ask: "What ever made you marry me in the first
place?"
"How do you expect me to answer a question like that?"
"I don't know. Perhaps I should go off on a trip. I feel in the mood for it."

78. *Zenshū*, 5: 81.
79. *Zenshū*, 5: 89.

"But why?" she would ask, flabbergasted. "Only the other day, after you'd been out somewhere, you said there was no better place than home. You seem to change your mind rather quickly these days."

She tried telling herself that her husband was playing the fool, but it was no good. She became nervous and irritated.

It began to be hot. As they had done the previous year, they brought out their good clothes from storage and hung them out to air in the sun. There were the dresses she had brought with her from home, which she had no opportunity to wear in this country town. There were the formal clothes they had worn at the wedding. And there was the sash that Sankichi's elder brother, Minoru, had given her as a wedding present and which she had never worn. They were now all swaying gently before her eyes in the breeze. She thought sadly: "I don't need them any more."

Her child was by her side, sleeping in the summer dress her mother had sent. She lay down dutifully with a sigh and waking the child, began to nurse it. With longing she looked again at the clothes outside.[80]

Their relationship has changed little when, after living in the country town for seven years, Sankichi decides to move with his family—they now have three daughters—to Tokyo. There still seems to exist a kind of love between the couple, but it is marred by the presence of mutual resentment and aloofness. Sankichi has been working on a long book for a year or so, and he hopes to complete it in Tokyo and publish it at his own cost. With money borrowed from a friend and from his father-in-law, Sankichi once more returns to the capital for an extended stay. They have rented a small house on the outskirts of the city.

At about four o'clock in the afternoon, the five arrived at Shinjuku Station. Since they were going to have to live frugally until his work was finished, they had no maid with them. The two older children seemed cheerful enough and looked about brightly as they walked beside their parents. But the youngest, who was being carried on Oyuki's back, seemed quite exhausted by the journey. She rested her head quietly on her mother's shoulder; and her eyes were dull and still. Occasionally Oyuki would stop and, pointing to something interesting, say to the child: "Look at that!" But there would be no response. Spring had just come to this suburb of Tokyo. They could now see, through the young leaves, the shingle roof of their house shining in the sun.[81]

The youngest child is ill. Shortly after, she dies; and her sisters do not survive her for long. Yet even in the face of such misfortune, Sankichi and Oyuki cannot come closer to each other.

80. *Zenshū*, 5: 106–7.
81. *Zenshū*, 5: 206.

Perhaps the fault is mostly Sankichi's. He cannot bring himself to communicate his sorrow or his loneliness to Oyuki. We see him talking openly to Shōta but never to his wife. Oyuki, on her part, can only interpret her husband's aloofness as a sign of indifference; and in self-defense perhaps, she does not reveal much warmth or understanding. This lack of communication between the two lasts for years. But in his own way Sankichi never ceases to love Oyuki. Many years after the incident of the letters, Tsutomu, who has become more or less a friend of the family, comes up to Tokyo on business and pays them a visit. Sankichi observes him and Oyuki carrying on an easy and cheerful conversation and becomes bitterly jealous. The intensity of his own emotion shocks and shames Sankichi. "He then came to realize," Tōson writes, "that he had really never forgiven them."[82]

Slowly Sankichi begins to act with less aloofness towards Oyuki. One day, he goes so far as to take her out on a shopping spree and then to a European-style restaurant. Oyuki makes no comment. But Sankichi with wry amusement notes the incredulity in her eyes. This rare act of generosity on Sankichi's part has been prompted by his incredibly childish decision, made immediately after the discovery of his own capacity for jealousy and resentment, to cleanse himself of all such emotions and to treat Oyuki kindly as though she were his younger sister. Tōson himself offers us no explicit evaluation of this strange decision. But in his description of the end of the outing, we find what might otherwise have been a wholly melancholic passage closing on an incongruous yet touching note of self-derision:

> The sun was about to set. And gradually the scene outside, framed by the windows of the restaurant, began to sink into darkness. The two left the restaurant. Sankichi, looking very much like a man who was trying fearfully to rebel against his own pessimism, took his replete "younger sister" home.[83]

It is finally Oyuki and not Sankichi that opens the way to greater understanding between the two. Shōta's wife, Toyose, has been visiting her; after she has gone, Oyuki comes into Sankichi's study to talk to him about Toyose and Shōta.

> "And do you know what Toyose said to me before she left? She said, 'I really do envy you, aunt.'"

82. Zenshū, 5: 363.
83. Zenshū, 5: 367.

"But you've always given me the impression," said Sankichi sharply, "that you're far from contented."

"You're quite mistaken," Oyuki said. Sankichi was impressed by the positiveness of her tone. He looked at her for a while.

"We have nothing that Toyose can be envious of," he said. "Except good health, I suppose." He picked up his pen and went back to work.

That night the two talked for a long time about Shōta and Toyose. Then shortly after the children seemed at last to have gone to sleep, Oyuki suddenly said: "Please trust me. Please, say that you trust me." She buried her face in his shoulder and began to weep quietly.

"It's too late now to start talking about trust," he was about to say, but the words did not come out. In silence, and with a mixture of regret and happiness, he listened to his wife weep.[84]

And so as the novel approaches its end, a measure of hope comes to the couple. Perhaps they at least will survive as a family. Three more children have been born to them since the death of their first three, and another is on the way. Soon after giving birth to this child, Oyuki will die. But the tragic irony of their marriage—that she should die just as they are beginning to find contentment in their life together—is to be described in *A New Life*. In the last scene of *The House*, we see them talking gently to each other about their relations and about themselves. It is a very hot and still night, and they cannot go to sleep. That day over in Nagoya, Shōta has died, and the cremation will take place some time during the night. Remarking to Oyuki that it should soon be daylight, Sankichi walks over to the storm window and slides it open. The novel closes as he looks out into the darkness, wondering whether they have already burned Shōta's body.

.

A New Life

Tōson began writing *A New Life* in 1918 and finished it in 1919. It is an altogether different kind of novel from *The House*, in that it is an account of a single major experience in the author's private life. It is a confession, or a justification perhaps, of his illicit relationship with one of his nieces. Unlike *The House*, therefore, it is the kind of novel that demands, by the very nature of its content, a ruthless and articulate examination of the state of mind

84. *Zenshū*, 5: 429–30.

of the characters involved. Not surprisingly, it is as conspicuous a failure as *Spring*. Tōson is so heavyhandedly circuitous in his treatment of the delicate subject matter that we begin to find ourselves in sympathy with Akutagawa Ryūnosuke who, on reading it, was moved to comment that he had never encountered anyone so hypocritical as its hero.[85]

Kishimoto (Tōson once more calls himself by that name) is in his early forties and has been a widower for almost three years. His household now consists of two young sons, Senta and Shigeru, an elderly maid, and a grown niece, Setsuko, who acts as both housekeeper and a kind of governess.[86] It is a measure of Tōson's vagueness that for the first forty pages or so, he gives us no recognizable indication that there is anything unusual in the relationship between the uncle and niece; instead, he gives us a lengthy and very serious-minded discourse on Kishimoto's disillusionment with life in general. As the book opens, we see Kishimoto coming away from the funeral of an old school friend, and thinking of all those close to him who have died. He begins to brood over his own loneliness, and wonders whether there is any purpose left in his life.

> He began to lose all pleasure in living. Was it the result of having worked too hard? Or was it simply another of those fits of depression that he had suffered intermittently since his youth? Or was it sheer fatigue from having had to take care of his motherless children these past three years? He could not say.[87]

He thinks often of his dead wife:

> He could still hear Sonoko [i.e., Oyuki of *The House*] crying on his shoulder and saying: "Please trust me. Please, say that you trust me."
> He had waited twelve years for those words. Sonoko was not like other girls from rich houses: she bore hardship without complaint, and she liked to work. She had many qualities which would have made any husband happy. But she had come to Kishimoto with a past that gave him cause to be terribly jealous. And it was a long time before he realized that he had been too hard on her. It was after twelve years of living together, he would now think with regret, that they were able to reach true understanding. And then she was dead.
> Kishimoto could not bear to listen to talk of a second marriage. He simply was not ready to marry again. His own single state had come to be for him a

---

85. *Akutagawa Ryūnosuke zenshū*, 10 vols. (Tokyo, 1934–35), 5: 582.
86. There is another son, who is living with Kishimoto's elder sister in Kiso, and a daughter who is living with an old nurse. These two children do not appear in the novel. Setsuko is the girl whom we encountered as Onobu in *The House*.
87. *Zenshū*, 6: 12.

kind of revenge on womankind. He had become afraid of even the thought of loving another woman: his experience of loving had hurt him so much.[88]

Such preliminary description of Kishimoto's condition is not in itself objectionable. But the reader quite naturally asks in what way it is intended to illuminate the nature of Kishimoto's relationship with his niece. That is, when the story actually begins with the sudden announcement by Setsuko that she is pregnant, the surprised reader is forced to presume that Tōson has, in the course of the preceding forty pages, somehow been trying to provide a basis for understanding why Kishimoto had seduced her. Was he having his revenge on womankind? But surely we are not expected to believe that an intelligent, mature man will seduce a girl twenty years his junior, and his niece at that, for so flamboyant a reason? Besides, we have not been quite convinced of the reality of this peculiar desire for revenge in the first place. Did he, then, seduce his niece because he was disillusioned with life? But without further clarification, such an explanation would be so obscure as to be absolutely meaningless. In short, Tōson offers us no intelligible explanation as to why or in what circumstances the unfortunate relationship was allowed to begin. And not unreasonably, we come to the conclusion that in the first few chapters of the book Tōson, whether consciously or unconsciously, is attributing to Kishimoto motives which are highly unrealistic. That Kishimoto was not in love with Setsuko becomes quite clear in the course of the novel. Perhaps he was simply lonely and needed a mistress; or perhaps living under the same roof with an unattached young woman proved too much of a temptation. But no such straightforward reason is given by Tōson.

Unfortunately, the whole novel abounds in obfuscations of this sort. And when judged in the light of what we presume to have been Tōson's primary intention of writing it—that is, to write a "confessional" novel[89]—it is an obvious failure. For in such a novel as this, where self-examination is the chief concern of the author, a vague accounting for one's actions is inexcusable.

But it is not without its redeeming qualities. Despite the annoying lack of self-understanding that the author seems to

88. *Zenshū*, 6: 30–31.
89. That Tōson intended *A New Life* to be a "confession" seems beyond question. In the latter half of the book, the word *zange* (confession) appears frequently.

manifest throughout the novel, for all the naïve and transparent posing, *A New Life*, perhaps because of the very solemnity of the content, invites our respect. And it is evidence of Tōson's peculiar strength as a writer that even the clumsiness, which becomes so conspicuous in his more explicit attempts to explain the conduct of his characters, begins to seem a necessary part of his individuality. At any rate, he does manage, in his tenacious fashion, to make the prolonged emotional ordeal that Kishimoto undergoes real enough for the reader. Moreover, in all those passages where Tōson's intention is to limit the reader's attention to the immediate, he writes unerringly. Here is the description of the fateful moment when Setsuko tells her uncle of her pregnancy:

> One evening Setsuko, close by Kishimoto's side, suddenly blurted out: "Uncle, you know what's the matter with me, don't you?"
> New Year's Day was just past, and Setsuko was now twenty-one. The two boys were in the house opposite, playing; the maid was out too, having gone to fetch the boys. She was obviously staying on to gossip. There was no one downstairs. In a whisper, Setsuko went on to say that she was going to be a mother.
> A shiver went through Kishimoto. It was as though the moment he had been trying desperately to postpone had finally come. Setsuko had only whispered; she had spoken quietly and unwillingly, like a person who had tried but could no longer keep the secret to herself; yet her words seemed to beat against his eardrums with frightening force. He could not remain with his niece, who sat there in utter dejection. He spoke a few words of comfort to her, then quickly left her side. He still felt shivery as he crept down the stairs. He sat down in his room, holding his head.[90]

Kishimoto's behavior hereafter is quite abject. Fear of censure and derision becomes, it would seem, the sole basis of all he does. In his frantic search for some way of averting disgrace, Setsuko is all but forgotten. His primary concern now is not how Setsuko may be protected from whatever unkindness she will be exposed to, but how he himself may avoid the acute embarrassment of having to face up to her family, in particular her father Yoshio (Morihiko in *The House*). There are not many alternatives. Abortion? Suicide? But surely, there must be a less extreme course of action open to him? Finally, he hits upon a solution which, from his point of view, is the only practicable one. He will run away.

90. *Zenshū*, 6: 39.

The idea first comes to Kishimoto, we are told, when a friend innocently says to him that he should go abroad. They are at a restaurant, and they have been drinking. He begins to ponder over the chance remark made by his companion. "In the course of the evening, Kishimoto, ordinarily a sober man, became unusually drunk. As the evening wore on, he felt his mind growing strangely clearer and more active. He said to himself: 'That was a good suggestion my friend here made. I simply can't take any more. I must do something or I'll be destroyed.' "[91] He goes home resolved to leave the country. To Setsuko, who lets him into the house, he has this to say: "I have something good to tell you. Wait till the morning."[92]

We cannot help wondering by what devious process of rationalization Kishimoto has arrived at the conclusion that Setsuko would welcome the prospect of being deserted by her lover. Does Tōson intend us here to see the heartlessness and irrationality of Kishimoto? Or does he really believe that Kishimoto's decision to go away is at least in part prompted by a certain selfless regard for Setsuko's welfare? We are not sure; and we have the uncomfortable feeling that neither is Tōson.

The next morning, Kishimoto finds that his resolution of the night before has remained unshaken. Without the slightest suggestion of criticism Tōson writes: "Leave everything behind, he told himself, and go across the seas. Go somewhere you've never been, amongst people you don't know. There, you can hide your shame. And perhaps, by this act of self-punishment, you can save Setsuko."[93]

Kishimoto begins immediately to prepare for the coming journey. He will go to France and stay there indefinitely. He lets it be known to his acquaintances that he is going largely for the sake of self-improvement. And when Setsuko's father, Yoshio, who has been living in Nagoya, comes to Tokyo on business, Kishimoto simply cannot bring himself to tell him about his daughter. The unsuspecting brother enthusiastically approves of Kishimoto's plan to go abroad and agrees to look after the two boys while their father is away. Kishimoto will rent a large house before he leaves. Yoshio, his wife, their two youngest children,

91. *Zenshū*, 6: 67.
92. *Zenshū*, 6: 69.
93. *Zenshū*, 6: 70.

and his mother-in-law will all come to Tokyo and live in the new
house with Setsuko and Kishimoto's sons.

> After his brother had left, Kishimoto called Setsuko into his room and tried
> to give some comfort to her troubled mind by telling her what her father had
> said.
>
> "But I simply couldn't tell him about you. I simply didn't have the face to
> ask him to take care of you when the time came." He sighed. "And what a
> shock it will be for your mother," he went on to say, "when she comes to
> Tokyo and finds out."
>
> Kishimoto thought of the friendly way in which Yoshio had encouraged him
> to go abroad. To have postponed mentioning his offense to him, then to have
> had the gall to ask him to look after his two sons was, no matter how one looked
> at it, tantamount to having deceived him. And it was not only his brother
> that he was deceiving; he was deceiving his friends and everybody else. He
> could not help thinking what a pathetic act of falsehood his decision to go abroad
> was. News of his impending departure was spreading; and as more and more
> people were taken in by his story that he was going merely in the capacity of a
> student-at-large, the greater his burden of guilt seemed to become. He must
> leave as quietly as possible, he thought. He would say goodbye only to those
> people that he knew well. And then, after he had left, he could try to make up
> for what he had done by suffering. But there was one thing he had to do before
> leaving, and that was to ask Yoshio to take good care of Setsuko. The mere
> thought of it filled him with shame.[94]

His sister-in-law Kayo (she has only a minor role in *The House*)
frightens him even more than his brother. He cannot bear to
think of the day when Setsuko will be exposed to her mother's
practised eye. Knowing full well that he is being unforgivably
rude to Kayo, who has arranged to come to the capital in time
to see him off, he departs for Kobe, the port of embarkation, days
before the sailing date in order to avoid meeting her. Once
there, distance will afford him some protection against the fury
of his sister-in-law when she discovers what he has done to her
daughter.

Whatever we may say of Tōson's seeming lack of awareness
throughout the novel, there is no doubting the honesty of his
treatment of Kishimoto's behavior here. What he tells us about
Kishimoto is so shameful and yet so true that for a moment at
least, we cease to feel detached contempt for Kishimoto and
begin to feel acutely ashamed ourselves. *A New Life* is thus a
strangely inconsistent work. Much of the time it leaves us

skeptical, if not incredulous, but sometimes it succeeds in forcing us to share in the guilt and shame of the protagonist, which is perhaps what a "confessional" novel of this sort ought to do.

He stays at a hotel in Kobe for two weeks, impatiently waiting for the day when he may at last seek the sanctuary of a ship.

These two weeks seemed to him to pass very slowly. He had managed to leave Tokyo, and he was now in Kobe, far away from Setsuko. Yet the distance he had put between himself and her was not sufficient to give him any sense of security. They were chasing him, he felt, and if he didn't get away soon, he would be caught. He was in constant terror lest that day, or the next, he should hear from Tokyo.[95]

And when one afternoon Yoshio suddenly turns up at the hotel, he is sure his guilty secret has been discovered and is panic-striken. But Yoshio is his usual cheerful self. He has come down from Nagoya, he says, to bid his younger brother *bon voyage* in person; besides, he has some business to attend to in Kobe. He chats away for a few minutes, then with his characteristic abruptness gets up to leave. Kishimoto's conscience warns him that this is his last opportunity of telling his brother about Setsuko. But he is too fearful and ashamed. "And so in the end Kishimoto said nothing as they parted. He thought of his offense, which was so grave he dared not ask forgiveness of his sister-in-law or his own brother, and sighed in despair."[96] He decides that he will write a letter of apology to Yoshio from the ship.

The day of the sailing finally arrives. "The time came," writes Tōson, "when he had to bear the burden of the secret sinner."[97] The journey at this point has become not an ignominious flight from responsibility but a self-inflicted punishment. And the letter which he writes to Yoshio as the ship nears Hong Kong is a strange mixture of honest apology and sentimental self-justification.

He wrote that Setsuko, whom Yoshio had so trustingly placed in his care, was now in a changed condition; that it was entirely his doing. He wrote that he had sometimes been obliged, for social reasons, to attend parties in places where wine was served, but, as his elder brother well knew, he had never ended up by doing anything he needed to be ashamed of; nevertheless, he had got himself into this shameful predicament. He wrote that in retrospect, he

95. *Zenshū*, 6: 101.
96. *Zenshū*, 6: 100.
97. *Zenshū*, 6: 104.

could see that his mistake had been to agree to take care of Setsuko, imagining that by doing so he could be of some assistance; that he had as a result ruined the life of an innocent girl and brought on himself such agony as he had never before known; that his offense was so great he had been unable to talk about it to his relations or to his friends. He wrote that Setsuko herself was guiltless and that he hoped Yoshio would forgive her; and that he had found the new house and asked Kayo to come to Tokyo simply in order to help Setsuko, to leave the girl in as secure a position as possible. He wrote also that he could hardly bear to imagine with what shock and sorrow Yoshio would read this letter; that he had lost all right to see Yoshio again, indeed even to write such a letter as this; that he was writing only for Setsuko's sake; and finally, that he was now going to a distant land to mourn the terrible unkindness of fate.[98]

A month later Kishimoto arrives in Paris, where he must live as an exile until such time as he feels prepared to face his relatives again. The first few days he passes in trepidation, waiting for word from Yoshio. At last the letter comes.

He trembled as he opened the letter. His elder brother, who was still living in Nagoya, had written it from Kishimoto's house in Tokyo. "I could not but feel despair," Yoshio wrote, "when I read your letter posted in Hong Kong. The thought of what you had done tormented me for days afterwards. Then I came up to Tokyo to make whatever arrangements were necessary. Before I say anything else, I will tell you this now: What is done is done, so try to forget about it.

"Since it is not the sort of thing one should talk about," he wrote, "I have made up my mind not to tell our mother, and not even Kayo. I shall tell Kayo that that person[99] has had an affair with a certain Mr. Yoshida and that this man has deserted her and disappeared. . . ."

Kishimoto gave a secret sigh of relief. He left his lodgings, a French language textbook tucked under his arm. He walked past the little fruiterer's shop and across the broad avenue, then past the old stone wall of the maternity hospital. He turned the corner when he reached the observatory. Soon he was at his tutor's house. After the lesson, he went back the same way towards his lodgings. He looked at the boys playing by the trees in front of the observatory and thought of his own children at home. He thought too of his own strange situation as he walked: here he was, a man of forty, taking elementary language lessons.

Kishimoto reread Yoshio's letter many times. There was no questioning his brother's generosity, and he was deeply grateful. A little of that dread, that oppressive feeling of being pursued, which had haunted him from Tokyo to Kobe, then to Shanghai and Hong Kong, and even as far as Paris, seemed at last to leave him.[100]

98. *Zenshū*, 6: 108–9.
99. Yoshio cannot bring himself to refer to his daughter by her name.
100. *Zenshū*, 6: 112–13.

Tōson's account of Kishimoto's three-year sojourn in France is perhaps the most satisfactory part of the book. It is here that Tōson's genius for description, which elsewhere in *A New Life* is almost completely obscured by his attempts at explanation, becomes most evident. In one important respect, indeed, the account is characteristically disappointing, for it fails to provide us with any additional insight into Kishimoto's motives; and at the end of it, we have no clearer picture of Tōson's attitude towards him than we ever had before. We were not certain how Tōson wished us to view Kishimoto's departure from Japan: was it to be understood as a shamefaced flight from the unpleasant consequences of a youthful *faux pas*, or was it a self-inflicted punishment in atonement for a serious moral offense? Similarly, Kishimoto's thoughts while in France are described with such vagueness, with such lack of formulation, that when he finally decides to end his exile, we are not sure exactly what considerations have led him to this decision. However, despite this serious failing, Tōson's description of Kishimoto's lonely sojourn in an alien country is a remarkably well sustained piece of good writing. Here, more than in any other section of the book, we are reminded that whatever his various shortcomings may be, Tōson is finally a writer of distinction. It is not strictly a narrative but rather a lyrical expression of the forlornness, the pathos, of an exile's condition. The following is a typical passage:

The most pleasant season in Paris arrived. Of those trees on the old dignified boulevards, the first to herald the coming of spring were the chestnut trees. Then the buds on the plane trees burst into leaf, and as the leaves grew larger and darker, the whole city, it seemed, became a world of green. One could see, over the stone fences, the hollies in the private gardens beginning to bloom; soon, their white and purple blossoms would be in full flower. It was a lovely time of the year, and Kishimoto felt his spirits reviving.

Yet, though he felt refreshed, he found that he could not relax. It was not that he had come to France with any thought of seeking a life of comfort. All he asked was that he be allowed to find peace of mind, which he needed so much. But so far he had not found it. Why could he not feel, he asked himself, that all he had done was to move his study temporarily from Tokyo to the boarding house in Paris? Slightly irritated at himself, he left his room and went outside. The plane trees by the maternity hospital cast their shadows on the sidewalk. A group of schoolboys with their teacher walked past, bathed in the warm sunshine. They were probably on their way to a picnic. Their French eyes were full of curiosity as they looked at Kishimoto. He stood and watched these innocent boys and thought of his own sons far away. Shigeru, the younger one, was now in his first year at school. Kishimoto imagined him walking to school with his brother Senta.

He walked towards the observatory. There too he found little children. They were playing in the shade of the tall, calm chestnut trees. High above were the flowers, full blown; and it seemed to Kishimoto that these were stage lights, casting their gentle glow on the spring scene below.

Fresh memories came back to him of the time he arrived in Marseilles and stepped onto European soil for the first time in his life. He felt as though he had never stopped walking since. Remaining indoors under the roof of a French tenement was to him little different from walking in his leather shoes on the cold stone pavements of Paris. He could not find true rest anywhere. He had gone to parks, stood in front of shop windows, sat down in strange coffee shops, not because he wanted to but simply because there had been nothing else for him to do. There had been periods when he would wander in this aimless fashion for days on end. Indeed, one could say he had spent the entire year in this alien land like a lost child. What a way to live, he thought, with a touch of incredulity.

When he got back to his room he was quite exhausted by the long walk under the fresh young leaves. He had seen so many streets that day. He went to the window and stood there, utterly forlorn. Far away in the sky were fluffy white clouds like those he remembered seeing from the mountains of Shinshū. Blown about by the early spring breeze, they changed their shape endlessly. He watched them, alone, with no one beside him to share his thoughts. The work he had brought with him from Japan lay on his desk untouched. But there were his children in Tokyo that he had to support; he must somehow get down to work. I have become homesick, he thought disgustedly. He felt the strain of exile so acutely then that he could have thrown himself onto the bare wooden floor and wept.[101]

A few months later, the World War begins. His life is changed little by the great event, as far as we can gather. He flees to the provinces for a short while, then returns to Paris and resumes his solitary life there. He remains for two more years, at the end of which period he finally decides to end his exile.

That night he climbed into his bed late. He did not try to go to sleep immediately; he propped himself up on his elbow and began to think of the days of his youth and of the friends he had then. It was almost twenty years ago, he remembered, that Aoki had died so young; he had outlived him that long. He thought of his life since. He had tried throughout to retain the simplicity of spirit of his childhood. Now, he was near to losing that simplicity. He said to himself: "I must at all costs find a way of returning to it." That night, there was more youthful hope in his heart than there had ever been since he left Japan.

Kishimoto's stubborn mind gradually began to change. If he were to decide not to go home and were to commit himself totally to living among these

101. *Zenshū*, 6: 142–44.

strangers, what could he do with his life? France was at war; all Frenchmen
between the ages of eighteen and forty-nine were serving their country. . . .
He could, he supposed, join up as a volunteer if he really wanted to. But why
push himself so far? Why go so much out of his way to stay in France and continue to cause his children at home so much unhappiness? It was when he reached
this point in his thinking that he at last made up his mind to go home.[102]

Later he adds, a little weightily: "To find the strength to live
in the midst of death—that was the wish not only of the French
people around him, but his also. He longed for the coming of
spring."[103] Here again, Tōson fails to explain Kishimoto's motives
to our satisfaction. It is not that we are unwilling to grant that
perhaps the above considerations did in part motivate Kishimoto's
return; our objection, rather, is that Tōson seems here to exclude,
at least by implication, other likely considerations. We might
have been perfectly content, indeed, had Tōson simply allowed us
to conclude that after three years of the kind of loneliness Kishimoto has suffered, he would quite naturally feel that he must go
home.

The second half of the book deals with Kishimoto's relations
with Setsuko and her family after his return. Despite his great
relief at seeing Japan again, there is still the air of the fugitive
about him as he arrives in Tokyo. His long absence, after all,
was only a temporary escape and not a real solution. He knows
that Setsuko's mother, Kayo, has never been told the truth.
What she has been told—though in fact she does not believe it—
is that Setsuko's illegitimate baby, which was born shortly after
Kishimoto's departure and which was immediately given
away, was fathered by some faithless lover. Setsuko herself has
remained unmarried; what does she expect of Kishimoto now?
As for Yoshio, can he really be as forgiving as he seemed in his
letter?

For fear of being seen by someone who knows him, he gets
off the train at Shinagawa and not at the main Tokyo terminus.
It is a lonely and furtive homecoming.

As he stood outside the deserted station building, he began at last to feel that
he had come home. This lonely return to the capital seemed to him an appropriate way to end the long, ignoble interlude.

102. *Zenshū*, 6: 233–34.
103. *Zenshū*, 6: 237.
10—T.J.N.

He forgot how very tired he was. The rickshaw he had ordered now appeared, and he got into it; the luggage would be sent on separately. Soon the rickshaw was zigzagging up the steep road that had been newly opened between Shinagawa and Takanawa. It was a bright July day. The sun had never been as clear as this in Paris, he thought: the sky there had always seemed muddy. The hood was up, but everything he looked at glittered so much that he felt as though his brain was being pierced by the sharp, powerful light. As the rickshaw drew nearer and nearer to his house, the faces of those waiting for him grew more vivid in his mind and became confused with the harsh images of the passing scene that beat against his eyes. He was filled with anxiety. Distressing as the prospect of seeing Yoshio and Kayo was to him, what worried him far more was the thought of Setsuko; he could hardly bear to think of all the misery his own immorality had caused her and what her experiences during his absence must have done to her.

The panting rickshaw man suddenly became more energetic. They had finally reached the top of the hill. Kishimoto was very near home now, and he could not help wishing that the man would go more slowly. They turned into a side-street. At the corner was the tobacconist's, and Kishimoto thought he saw his younger son playing in front of it. He suddenly found himself calling: "Shigeru! Aren't you Shigeru?"

The boy had grown almost beyond recognition. He hardly looked at the hooded rickshaw. Mysteriously he answered: "Papa isn't back yet!" Then he rushed down the street towards the house, shouting something joyfully. Kishimoto could see, by this time, the gate of his house.[104]

Yoshio gives him a warm welcome; we wonder, however, whether it is entirely sincere. Kayo too appears pleased, but Kishimoto senses a certain bitterness in her, and he begins to suspect that she has somehow guessed the truth. Setsuko's manner is withdrawn and strained. It is altogether a strange family reunion. The occasion must after all be acknowledged to be a happy one; and everything that is said is friendly to the point of being hearty. Yet beneath the surface jollity and solicitousness, there is the scarcely concealed undercurrent of mutual suspicion and resentment. "An atmosphere of desperate suppression seemed to pervade the house," Tōson writes. "Even the expression on the children's faces seemed to Kishimoto to be stiff."[105]

Kishimoto and his two sons must live for a while with their relations until the latter find a house of their own. It is during this short period when they are all living under one roof that Kishimoto and Setsuko repeat their old mistake. Kishimoto, however, is not the man he was before, we are told; and so his reasons for

104. Zenshū, 6: 266–67.
105. Zenshū, 6: 269.

seducing his niece have also changed. "He had ceased," Tōson says, "to regard his own unmarried state as a kind of revenge on women; he no longer hated them so much." This comment is followed, not many lines later, by yet another abstraction: "In Kishimoto's breast there had begun to grow a profound sense of pity, a desire to save not only Setsuko but himself also."[106] This time, then, Kishimoto becomes Setsuko's lover not for the sake of revenge but through some desire for mutual salvation.

From this point on until we reach the end of the novel, Tōson treats the whole problem of their relationship as though it were a religious experience. Unfortunately, he makes very little effort to convince us that Kishimoto is in any normally accepted sense in love with Setsuko. Rather, he almost blatantly presents Kishimoto in the role of a generous guardian, selflessly dedicating himself to the improvement of his ward's condition. We are led to infer that their relationship is an ennobling one for both Kishimoto and Setsuko. But since we never come to know Setsuko as a personality in her own right and since Kishimoto's attitude towards his mistress seems devoid of love, it is inevitable that our reaction should be tinged with skepticism.

The two continue to see each other after Setsuko and her parents have moved out of Kishimoto's house. They do not have to meet in secret, for Kishimoto's suggestion that Setsuko become his secretary is welcomed by both Yoshio and Kayo, who have for some time disapproved of their unmarried daughter's aimless and dependent existence.

> Kishimoto decided that he would try to teach Setsuko, who had to rely on her parents for support, some way of becoming more independent. He felt that even if she were to continue to live as she had done, without any change in her status, she should at least be encouraged to earn some money she could call her own. She could perhaps learn to take down dictation and do other things too that would be of help to him in his work. In return he would pay her a regular salary. He wanted not only to teach her to earn money but to give her a purpose in life.
>
> When he spoke about his idea to Yoshio and Kayo, they were both delighted.[107]

Such a situation, however, cannot last indefinitely. They cannot marry each other, nor, so long as they remain lovers,

106. *Zenshū*, 6: 302.
107. *Zenshū*, 6: 303.

can they marry anyone else. Moreover, the strain of having to keep their unnatural relationship a secret becomes more and more oppressive to Kishimoto. Finally, he decides he cannot go on lying about himself and Setsuko. He will write his "confession" and publish it. (The work in question is of course *A New Life*.) Setsuko, he is sure, will welcome his decision. She is not the bitter, resentful girl that she was when he first returned from France. She has matured considerably under his tutelage and has learned to depend on herself. ("I think," says Kishimoto to her on one occasion, "that all the suffering you've gone through hasn't been in vain. I think it's made you a better person in the end.") [108] And so once more we see Kishimoto's curious reasoning at work:

> Kishimoto now arrived at the stage where he felt he had to escape from the shamefaced, fearful, convict-like existence he had been leading and begin to live an open, free life again. . . . He realized that though he had tried hard to atone for his past sins, he had never tried to rid his life of falsehood. True, his desperate efforts so far to hide his guilty secret had been as much for Setsuko's sake as his; but such concern for Setsuko had become meaningless, now that there was this new understanding, this new sympathy between them. He came to believe, indeed, that to bring their secret out into the open would not hurt Setsuko, but instead help her find her way to a life of truth. [109]

As he begins to write his book, he finds a new peace of mind. Its publication will no doubt cause a scandal. And Yoshio of course will never forgive him or Setsuko. But he is prepared to accept, if need be, ostracization by the entire family. He is certain that Setsuko is no less prepared to pay whatever price will be demanded of her by her family and society at large. Under his encouragement, she has of late begun to seek solace in religious meditation. Her new religious outlook will give her the needed strength.

> Kishimoto felt that Setsuko was no longer in need of him. She was ready to stand on her own feet. That much she had learned from him, at any rate. He had always thought of her as being very young, but she was now twenty-six. If she really wanted to pursue a religious life, he would do whatever was possible to help her get her wish. He would continue to support her financially, as he had been doing regularly every month for some time past, so that she would not lack any of the necessities. [110]

108. *Zenshū*, 6: 305.
109. *Zenshū*, 6: 401.
110. *Zenshū*, 6: 437.

Yoshio is given no warning of the impending publication of his brother's new book. We cannot but wonder how Kishimoto can, with such blandness, behave quite so badly towards Yoshio. And we are inclined to agree with the latter when, upon the publication of the first part of the novel, he sends this message to Kishimoto: "What a sorry business writing must be, when in order to eat you have to wash your dirty linen in public."[111]

The relationship between Setsuko and Kishimoto is now over. Yoshio will never permit them to see each other again. Setsuko will join her uncle Tamisuke (Minoru in *The House*) in Taiwan, and there live, we presume, the life of a religious recluse. It is a terrible predicament, yet it fails to affect us very deeply. Try as we may, we cannot bring ourselves to take her any more seriously than Kishimoto seems to have done throughout the novel.

Before the Dawn

Tōson began working on *Before the Dawn*, his last completed novel, in 1927 and finished it in 1935. It has some conspicuous imperfections: it is even more loosely constructed than *The House*; it is written in a style so bereft of ornament that its determined inelegance sometimes begins to seem unnecessary; it is too frequently interrupted by extended historical discourses on the main events surrounding the Meiji Restoration; and of the many characters that appear in it, not one, not even the hero, seems to emerge as a fully rounded personality. Yet, for all its faults, *Before the Dawn* seems to deserve its fame. Indeed, it has two qualities so rarely to be found in modern Japanese fiction that their presence alone seems to give it a unique distinction. These two qualities are grandeur and a genuine sense of tragedy.

The scope of the novel is ambitious. The main intention of Tōson here is to trace the life of his father, whom he calls Hanzō, and to depict him as an idealist and a dedicated reformer whose hopes are inevitably destroyed by the ugly realities of the Meiji Restoration. But also, in the course of his depiction of Hanzō as a tragic figure betrayed by his own times, Tōson is careful to

---

describe in great detail not only those major national events that took place in Japan during the years immediately before and after the Restoration, but the social conditions prevailing in the relatively remote Kiso Valley area at the time. *Before the Dawn*, then, is more than a novel written in piety by a son who had never really known his father; it is also an attempt to see the vast social and political upheaval which came to be known as the Meiji Restoration through his father's eyes.

Magome is a village on the Kiso Road (Kiso-ji),[112] one of the five main highways of feudal Japan. The village, though situated in the mountainous Kiso Valley region behind Nagoya, is a relatively important one, for it is an officially designated stopping place for travellers on the highway. The Aoyama, who have records clearly dating back some three hundred years, are the leading family of Magome. Indeed, there seems little doubt that an ancestor of theirs, a man of gentle birth who had for some reason come to this remote region seeking refuge, founded the village. They have for generations held the two important village posts of *shōya* and *honjin*. As *shōya* the head of the Aoyama house is directly answerable to the *daikan* (the local domanial official) at Kiso Fukushima for the proper administration of village affairs; and as *honjin*, he must act as host to the travelling daimyo, *bakufu* (shogunal government) officials, *kuge* (court noble) emissaries, and other men of rank who would stop at Magome for a meal or even a night's stay, and maintain a household large enough to meet the needs of such dignitaries. He owns a substantial amount of land in and around the village, and thirteen peasant families look to him as their squire. Shortly before his retirement, Hanzō's father, Kichizaemon, is given, presumably as a matter of course, formal permission to use his family name, wear two swords, and to request an audience with the great Owari daimyo himself at the castle in Nagoya. The Aoyama, therefore, are a family of considerable importance locally.

When the novel opens, Hanzō is eighteen and Kichizaemon is fifty-five. The year is 1853. The warm season has come and with it the dry days. The villagers fear a drought, and decide to send two supplicants to the Grand Shrine of Suwa.

112. This is another name for the Nakasendō.

It was while the people of Magome were thus engaged in prayer-offering that they heard of the appearance of numerous black ships off Uraga on the Tōkaidō.

Kudayū, the commission agent, first heard about it from the courier from Edo, west-bound for Hikone. He passed the news on to Kichizaemon and to Kimbei [a wealthy merchant and Kichizaemon's friend and neighbor]. According to Kudayū, the courier was carrying an order from the *bakufu* to the lord of Hikone, telling him to report for duty at once.

By the time the two supplicants returned from Suwa, the courier had hurried off into the dry, summer night. This was on the tenth of June, 1853. Even a fast courier would take days to get to this remote mountain village on the Nakasendō from Edo. At the time, therefore, all that the villagers vaguely heard was that several black ships, sent by some foreign power, had suddenly appeared in Japanese waters. How were they to know that these were in fact four American battleships, led by Commodore Perry on his first visit to Japan?

Kimbei whispered to Kichizaemon: "Edo, I hear, is in turmoil." This was all he knew.[113]

The Tokugawa *bakufu* has received its deathblow, and in another fifteen years the emperor will be restored to power. The people of course do not know that the old order will soon come to an end. Yet the signs of its decay are becoming increasingly obvious, and such men as Kichizaemon and his friend Kimbei, who are attached to the past, are deeply troubled by them. Not long after the coming of the black ships, the *bakufu* issues an order to the nation at large for gifts of money. It reaches Kichizaemon one day through the *daikan's* office in Kiso Fukushima. The family are in the midst of preparation for the coming marriage of Hanzō to Otami, a distant relation and the sister of the *honjin* of Tsumago, another station on the Kiso Road. Kichizaemon is in the family storehouse, making sure that there will be enough appropriate dinnerware for the wedding guests. A writ from Fukushima addressed to the *shōya* of Magome arrives at the main house. Kichizaemon's wife, Oman, takes it to him.

Oman could hear her husband moving about as she climbed the stairs to the second floor of the storehouse. When she saw him she said: "Here is a writ from Fukushima."

Kichizaemon, having found some free time for a change, was tidying up the second floor. Piled up against the walls were several old books, including his cherished collections of haiku and Chinese and Japanese classics. He took the document from Oman, and went to the window to read it.

The cost to the government, it said, of improving coastal defense would be enormous. Not only the three great cities of Edo, Kyoto, and Osaka, but the government estates in the various provinces and the most remote villages were being ordered to contribute funds. This was the time for all to express their gratitude to the government. Coastal defense had become an urgent consideration, it said, in view of the recent arrival, for the purpose of trade, of four American ships at Uraga and four Russian ships at Nagasaki.

Kichizaemon showed Oman the writ, saying: "The government wants contributions. It somehow seems wrong that we should be celebrating at a time like this. I shall have to do whatever I can to help. . . ."

After Oman had left, Kichizaemon once more went to the window. The November sun came through the iron bars and cast a gentle light all about him. He stood there, worrying about the writ from Fukushima. It was being secretly rumored that the *bakufu* had never been so poor, that there was no money left in its treasury. Kichizaemon was a conservative man, and he hated those people who went about spreading such rumors indiscriminately, not caring who heard them. He was concerned for his son, so young and still so impressionable. He did not want him to see too much of what went on beneath the official surface. Some day, Hanzō would be mature enough to bear knowing the ugly secrets between men. Until then, Kichizaemon thought, he ought to be allowed to harden gradually.[114]

Kichizaemon has noticed too that the recent increase in activity on the highways—daimyo and officials seem now to be constantly going to or coming from Edo—has affected the morals of the people in the area. Peasants from nearby settlements who have been conscripted to carry the luggage of the distinguished travellers and their trains have begun to pour into the village in great numbers, and among them are the inveterate gamblers and drinkers, who pass on their bad habits to others more innocent. In time, with the growing confusion and insecurity, many of the samurai also will lose their old restraint. "Now, whenever Kimbei met Kichizaemon, he would say: 'Things were different in the old days.' These two neighbors, who shared memories of Magome in the days gone by, could not forget the time when there was peace and security under the Tokugawa."[115]

Hanzō, however, does not feel the same attachment to the immediate past. It is not simply that he is much younger than Kichizaemon and Kimbei: he is ideologically opposed, not to the Tokugawa regime as such, but to the entire feudal system which, he believes, has been responsible for all the ills of Japanese society since the decline of imperial rule.

114. *Zenshū*, 7: 38–39.
115. *Zenshū*, 7: 66.

He is particularly conscious of the miserable condition of the peasants in and around Magome. As heir to the hereditary family posts of *shōya* and *honjin*, he is placed above the rest of the inhabitants of the rural community; but, at the same time, he is not of the samurai class. He may, then, either identify himself with the samurai and consider it his duty to serve as their representative placed among the peasantry; or he may choose to regard himself as a spokesman for the peasants and try to protect them as much as possible from the harsh demands of officialdom. He takes the latter course. "Though he was born heir to the ancient house of the Magome *honjin*," Tōson writes, "his sympathies were not with the powerful samurai officials placed above him but always with those docile, persevering peasants who did not even possess surnames."[116]

Very little of the mountainous region of Kiso is arable; and the only way the peasants there can live with any comfort at all is to be allowed access to the timber. The domanial authorities, however, though not entirely unsympathetic, are anxious to preserve the forests, and will allow the peasants only a fraction of the timber they need. In desperation, the peasants steal what they cannot get legally. Often, they are caught trespassing on the mountains, and they are punished.

When Hanzō was only eighteen, he witnessed the arrest of sixty-one men from the village for stealing timber. They were gathered together, handcuffed, in the courtyard of his house and there questioned by the officials who had come from Fukushima. He hid behind the pear tree at the end of the yard and watched. From that time on, his heart was always with the unfortunate, poverty-striken farmers and laborers.[117]

Life is particularly hard for those who must serve as porters whenever a dignitary travelling on the Nakasendō passes through. Whatever cash compensation they may receive can never make up for time lost on the farm. Nor does the rate of such compensation vary with the changes in the value of money or with the frequency in any given period of travellers needing assistance. The packs are heavy, the mountain paths steep, and sometimes, in extreme weather, an exhausted peasant will be left dying on the road. The Aoyama family suffers too, though of course not so

116. *Zenshū,* 7: 83.
117. *Zenshū,* 7: 82–83.

seriously: they must house and feed the lords and officials and their subordinates when they arrive; and when, as in the days immediately following Perry's arrival, the highway is busy, they begin to feel acutely the discrepancy between the payment they receive from the authorities and the actual cost of maintaining a *honjin*. Indeed, in the last years of the *bakufu*, the entire village of Magome is forced into a state of near-bankruptcy from having to fulfill its obligations as a station.

It is through his study of national literature and history, or *kokugaku*, that Hanzō finds a way of articulating his awareness of the hardships suffered by those who must serve the samurai:

> He was a disciple of Miyakawa Kansai of Nakatsugawa, a village not too distant from Magome. Kansai was a national scholar of the Hirata school. What this man taught Hanzō was the rejection of the middle ages and all that Japan had inherited from those dark times. Let us free ourselves, he said, from the authority of the Chinese scholars; let us cleanse our minds of all that the Buddhists have taught us. We must try to return to the innocent, kindly spirit of ancient times, when such alien ways of thought were yet unknown, and try to see things with fresh eyes. And so let us heed the teachings of those great men who paved the way of opposition for us: first there was Kada no Azumaro, who preceded them all; and then there were his successors, Kamo Mabuchi, Motoori Norinaga, and Hirata Atsutane.[118]

Hanzō has been taught to believe, therefore, that the social injustices he sees around him are not so much the fault of the Tokugawa rulers as the result of the artificial and rigid conventions that were introduced into Japan after the classical age. There will be happiness and justice in Japan only if the Japanese return to that simple and uncorrupted life depicted in the *Kojiki* and the *Manyoshū*. The excessively formal teachings of the Buddhists and the Chinese, so cherished by the military class, have all but destroyed the indigenous virtues of the Japanese people. Once, under the emperors, Japan was a happy country, where justice and mercy ruled, and there was no oppression. In those days the people, in their worship of the native gods, were able to give simple and spontaneous expression to their sense of gratitude for the gifts of this life. But later, the military, with their rigid and harsh way of life, and the schoolmen, with their alien learning, came and separated the people from the gods and the emperor. Then there was oppression from those that governed and fear in those that were governed. And in worship, the gay acceptance of the things of nature disappeared; now, shame has come to be attached even to love.

In Toson's view, such students of *kokugaku* as Miyakawa Kansai and Hanzō were not simply "nationalists." Rather, like reformers of other times and places, they believed, perhaps naïvely, that existing social ills could be cured by a return to the innocence of ancient times. If they were anti-foreign, they were so mostly because they imagined that it was through the introduction of alien ways that this innocence had been lost. And their sympathy for the imperial house was grounded partly on the assumption that with its restoration, the corrupt and oppressive institutions—social, religious, and bureaucratic—would disappear. They were of course idealists and were doomed to disappointment.

Hanzō's tragedy, then, is that being a student and reformer in the *kokugaku* tradition, he soon becomes an anachronism once the revolution has succeeded. For the ideals so cherished by him and his kind, no matter how useful they might have been to the political factions advocating the overthrow of the *bakufu* during its last declining years, soon come to be ignored by the post-Restoration bureaucrats.

Despite his attachment to the imperial cause, Hanzō is forced to stay in Magome throughout the eventful decade preceding the final overthrow of the *bakufu*. His friends and fellow students of *kokugaku* from the other villages of the area all leave for Kyoto to take part in the restoration movement. But he is Kichizaemon's only son and heir, and he must take over his father's duties when the latter resigns. He is an obedient son, and he accepts his fate quietly. Yet he cannot help feeling some bitterness over the unhappy prospect of living the rest of his life in Magome. One day, shortly before Kichizaemon officially resigns, Hanzō says to his wife: "You know, I've been apprenticed to my father since I was seventeen. But I'm not like your brother, I'm afraid. I cannot handle business matters. I don't enjoy keeping an exact record of how many people came here with some daimyo or other, what it cost the village to put them up, how many candles we had to use, and all that sort of thing. I'm rather a stupid fellow, as you see." [119]

From Magome, Hanzō watches the great events that are taking
place in distant Edo and Kyoto. Sometimes a letter from a friend
in Kyoto would arrive, describing the excitement there; or sometimes a traveller passing through would stop at the house and talk
to him of what he had seen. And very occasionally, Kiso itself,
or a place near it, would be the scene of some significant event,
and Hanzō would then be allowed to feel that he was not entirely
isolated from the great tide of reform that was sweeping the
country.

Such an event is the battle between the Mito rebels and the
local pro-*bakufu* forces at Wada Pass. The year is 1864. For over
two hundred years, there has been among the Mito clansmen a
widespread tradition of nationalism and of reverence for the
emperor, despite the fact that the domain has always been ruled
by one of the three major Tokugawa families. Until the middle of
the nineteenth century, this tradition has been largely academic in
nature. But with the coming of Perry, it turns quickly into an
active revolutionary ideal that offers a ready rationalization for
such acts of violence as the assassination in 1860 of Ii Naosuke, the
bakufu statesman, by the Mito *rōnin*. There is also, however, a
powerful pro-*bakufu* faction in Mito, which is after all a Tokugawa
clan. Feeling runs high on both sides, and finally, in 1864, there is
civil war in the domain. The pro-*bakufu* faction is victorious, and
the remnants of the defeated force, numbering about three
hundred clansmen and six hundred peasants, begin their march
westward, in the desperate hope that they may be allowed to seek
sanctuary in the western domain of Chōshū. There is no serious
effort to stop them until they get into Shinshū. There the two
minor clans of Suwa and Matsumoto, trusting that the *bakufu*
army in pursuit of the rebels will appear in time to aid them,
decide to combine forces and offer battle at Wada Pass.

Before sunrise the army of the Mito *rōnin* set out from Wada Station on the
Nakasendō. Takeda Kōunsai, titled Iga no kami, was their commander;
Tamaru Inaemon, who had been the city magistrate of Mito, was deputy
commander; and Yamakuni Hyōbu, who had been supervisor of pages at the
castle, and who was famed for his knowledge of military tactics, was chief of
staff. The *rōnin*, out of consideration for the peasant foot soldiers, had so far
limited the extent of their daily march to about ten miles. But that particular
day they would have to go up the steep mountain road for over eight miles
simply to reach the top of the pass.

It was a fine day. There was not a cloud in the morning sky. At last they reached the entrance to the pass. The long three-column line, tightly formed, slowly climbed the hill. In front fluttered their eight red-and-white banners. The houses near the top of the pass had been burned. They saw no sign of the enemy. As the advance guard on horseback neared the rock called Kōroiwa, four shots rang out from the woods above them. The bullets missed the horsemen, and hit the ground and the trees on the side of the road. Enemy soldiers were in the vicinity after all. On the top of the hill to the left men appeared and began signalling to the main Suwa force on the other side.

Large trees had been felled and laid across the road. Some of the Mito men began to go over these laboriously; others tried to remove them. The suspension bridge beyond had been severed, and this had to be mended. It was some time before the entire army was able to negotiate itself clear of the obstacles. A few of their number had managed to climb to the top of the hill above Kōroiwa and now hoisted a blue-and-white streamer. Then on the peak of the hill on the other side of the road, three red-and-white banners went up. The Mito men on these vantage points could look down and see the camp of the Suwa and Matsumoto clansmen.

The defending force had until this very moment been waiting for the *bakufu* army to appear. They could wait no longer; they had no choice but to fight the Mito men who were swarming down from the top of the pass and gathering fast on Hoshikusa Hill. Soon the two armies were facing each other across the valley, no more than five hundred yards apart. The Mito men were the first to open fire. The sound of the guns reverberated along the mountain tops and through the valley.

The Suwa contingent, who had agreed to bear the main brunt of the attack, fought well. Gradually the Mito men pressed down the hill, shouting their battle cry. They forced the defending troops back from Tozawaguchi towards Toihashi, but they were beaten back when the Suwa gunners began firing from behind their parapet. The Suwa and Matsumoto men were in a five-column formation. They had arranged their right wing in the standard fashion, with the gunners in front and the spearmen behind; but they had put the spearmen in front on their left wing; and every time the Mito men attacked, these spearmen would counterattack, shouting back their own battle cry. The Mito men tried to break through three times, but they failed.

The fighting had begun in the early afternoon. Sunset was approaching, and they had reached a stalemate. All either side could do was to continue firing on the enemy. But as the sun sank lower in the sky, the Mito men found themselves at a disadvantage; for the light shone directly into their eyes, and aiming became almost impossible. It was then that Yamakuni Hyōbu, the chief of staff, hit upon a plan. He knew well the geography of the area, having had a local guide explain it to him in detail. He ordered some of the men to drag a mortar up the hill to their right; and thus having distracted the enemy's attention, he had fifty or so men ford the stream to their left and ascend Mount Fukazawa. From this high point they fired on the flank of the Matsumoto contingent. Not only the Matsumoto clansmen but the Suwa clansmen were taken by surprise. The sun had gone down behind the mountains, and the Matsumoto men were exhausted. Then a bullet hit their captain, and confusion broke out. The fifty Mito men, seeing this, rushed down the mountainside, firing their small arms into the enemy ranks.

Takeda Kōunsai had moved his headquarters to Tozawaguchi. The moment had come for the final onslaught. He took up the war drum and began to beat it. It was dark. Some of the Suwa men were ready to retreat and showed concern lest the enemy should close in from the rear. The Suwa formation was still intact, however, and a few of the units were putting up a stubborn resistance at Toihashi. But once defeat was in the air, there was nothing anyone could do to stop the gradual disintegration of the ranks. They could not expect support from the Matsumoto men, who, it seemed, had no fight left in them. One after the other the Suwa men began to draw hastily away from the battle.

Thus it ended with the Suwa and Matsumoto forces in full flight. The *bakufu* army, on whose aid they had counted never came. The darkness was suddenly lit by bursting flames. The retreating army had set fire to the three farmhouses in Toihashi to rob the Mito men of shelter. Here and there, the bright light of the flames would show up the figure of some brave Suwa clansman who refused to run away. There was one man who rushed back to the guns in the entrenchment and fired twice at the pursuers. Skirmishes were still being fought between small, isolated units. Gradually the fires died down. It was about eight o'clock. There was no sign of the moon, now twenty days old, in the night sky. It had become impossible to distinguish between friend and enemy. The shapeless mass of the fleeing Suwa and Matsumoto clansmen disappeared into the darkness.[120]

Though the Mito men win this particular engagement, their future is quite hopeless. Behind them is the *bakufu* army and before them are unfriendly clans, far more powerful than Suwa or Matsumoto. As they approach Ōtsu, they learn that troops from the great clans of Kaga and Aizu and from other lesser clans have gathered there and are preparing for battle. They cannot fight against such odds, and they quickly surrender themselves to the officer commanding the Kaga force, in the hope that so powerful a clan as Kaga may be able to persuade the *bakufu* to be merciful. They are bitterly disappointed. The sentences passed on them by the *bakufu* are unexpectedly severe. Three hundred and fifty-three of the rebels are to be executed and two hundred and fifty exiled. Moreover, the sons of the three leaders, Takeda, Yamakuni, and Tamaru, are to be executed with their fathers, and the wives and daughters imprisoned for life. Tōson ends the episode with these words uttered despairingly by the gentle and

120. *Zenshū*, 7: 394–96.

aging Kichizaemon: "I am sixty-seven now, and I have lived too
long. I have seen too much."[121]

The *bakufu* may still be able to crush a minor, isolated rebellion,
but its power is nearly exhausted. The full extent of its decay
becomes all too evident in the following year, when it embarks
on the ill-fated second punitive expedition against the recalcitrant
Chōshū clan in western Japan. News of the campaign very rarely
reaches Magome, and when it does, it is vague and unreliable.

In the evening Hanzō visited his father who, since his retirement, lived on the
second floor of the cottage at the back of the main house. As soon as he saw his
son, Kichizaemon asked: "What news have you of the Chōshū expedition,
Hanzō?" In these troubled times, the old man could feel no more at rest than
his son. The sliding doors of the two-mat room had been taken out to let the
breeze in. The heat of the day still seemed to linger. Hanzō's stepmother Oman,
who had been helping in the main house all day, was now back and sat behind
Kichizaemon, massaging his back. Here in this room Kichizaemon was going
to live out his life just as his father, Hanroku, had done after retirement. Here
he would sit quietly day after day and think of the things that had happened in
the sixty-eight years he had lived on the Nakasendō.

"What is happening in the west?" Oman asked Hanzō, looking over
Kichizaemon's shoulder. Even she was interested.

"We can hardly expect news to travel very fast to these remote mountains,"
Hanzō said. "I really have no idea what is going on. We know that there was a
battle somewhere in the Kokura area. But that was some time ago. We've
heard nothing definite about what's happened since. Of course we are constantly hearing that the *bakufu* is sure to win, that an overwhelming victory is
imminent. But how can we take such vague, hopeful talk seriously?"[122]

Impatient to know what is really happening in the west,
Hanzō decides to go to Nagoya, the domanial capital, and solicit
information at the castle. It is an arduous journey on foot, for
Nagoya is fifty-five miles away. But once there, he is amply
rewarded for his trouble. From a quite trustworthy source, he
hears what he has for some time suspected, and perhaps hoped,
was the truth: the expedition has proved a disaster. He returns to
Magome and tells his father what he has heard.

"It would seem that the clans that joined the expedition were pretty half-
hearted about it from the start. There wasn't one clan, apparently, that really
wanted to fight Chōshū. I suppose they all supplied troops merely out of a
sense of obligation to the *bakufu*."

121. *Zenshū*, 7: 457.
122. *Zenshū*, 7: 480.

"But Hanzō, it's three months since the war began. Why, I've heard that there've been at least six or seven battles already."

"True enough, father. Yes, they've fought at Geishūguchi, for instance; and at Ōshima and Shimonoseki too. But these were all defensive battles. And they've done nothing but retreat. . . . I suppose the fact of the matter is no one wants to die for the *bakufu* any more. The primary concern of the various clans is apparently to see to it that they lose no more troops than is necessary. They've come to put their own individual interests before the *bakufu*'s, it seems."

"I suppose you're right. Take these peasant laborers now: you can't get them to work simply by telling them Lord Tokugawa wants them to."

"As for the officers at Nagoya Castle, they are wondering what in the world will happen next. The Owari clan was never in favor of the expedition, they are all saying angrily; had the *bakufu* listened to the advice of our old lord, they say, it would never have got itself into this mess. At any rate, rumor has it that Hamada Castle has fallen too. And what's more, I heard that the shogun was ill."

Kichizaemon heaved a deep sigh.[123]

Shortly thereafter Iemochi, the fourteenth Tokugawa shogun, dies. In 1867 his successor, Keiki, relinquishes the powers of government of the shogunate. The battles of Toba and Fushimi are yet to come, and there will be some fighting in Edo too. But the long awaited restoration of the emperor has taken place. The first part of *Before the Dawn*, then, ends as Hanzō hears from friends that what he has dreamed about for so many years has finally happened.

It is in a small teahouse on the road to Nakatsugawa, a village some miles distant from Magome, that he hears the good tidings. He is on his way to see Kōzō, a friend and fellow member of the Hirata school living in Nakatsugawa, to ask for news of Kyoto. As he is resting at the teahouse, Kōzō walks in, accompanied by Katsushige, a youth from another village in the area. Katsushige is a royalist sympathizer too, having studied *kokugaku* under Hanzō. They were going to Magome, they tell Hanzō, to bring him news of the end of Tokugawa government. The three order a meal, and talk together happily and at length of the great event.

The winter sun was out, and the teahouse was bathed in the warm light. When they had finished their meal, Hanzō and his friends went outside and walked about near the stone monument commemorating Bashō. He delighted in the feel of his straw sandals pressing firmly into the melting snow. His sense of well-being grew as he continued to walk. True, the real work of reform was yet to come. But this was the beginning. They were at last embarked on the great project of returning to the past, to the age of the gods. The mere thought of it filled him with awe.

He remembered once more those words of Hirata Atsutane's, which he had found in the master's writings and which had so impressed him:

"Surely, all is as the gods have willed."[124]

In the first part of *Before the Dawn*, then, Tōson seems to do little more than set the scene for what is to follow. Considered as an introduction, it is perhaps too long and meandering, written at too leisurely a pace. Too much of the content, it seems, deals with history, and too little with Hanzō. Yet the patient reader who continues on to the second part will in time decide that without the detailed background provided in the first part, the final fate of Hanzō will not have seemed half so moving or meaningful. The reason for this perhaps is that the great historical events which Tōson describes so carefully in the first part lend weight to Hanzō and increase his personal significance. Tōson does not, or cannot, depend on intimate portrayal of Hanzō to convince us of his tragedy. Even in the second part, Hanzō remains a vague figure: his relationship with his family or friends, his understanding of his own desires and fears, the cause of his final madness—these are only broadly stated or merely hinted at, and never explained to our full satisfaction. Rather, what seems to give power to Tōson's portrayal of Hanzō is the utter seriousness of the author's attempt to understand the times in which his father lived. Hanzō for Tōson has become almost a symbol: he is a dedicated idealist who is destroyed by a series of disillusionments. Tōson's memory of his father, one suspects, was little more complicated than this. And it may be for this reason that his characterization of Hanzō seems to us to be lacking in depth. However, a novel may be distinguished even if its protagonist is thinly drawn and its construction noticeably imperfect. It may possess, as *Before the Dawn* does, qualities which may fully compensate for such shortcomings. There is, we feel, great dignity in Tōson's devotion to the task he has set himself; and in the scale of the historical setting in which he has placed Hanzō, a certain magnificence. Thus we are persuaded of the significance of

Hanzō's predicament by the dignity with which he has been conceived and by the magnitude of the events that affect him.

Soon after the declaration of the restoration of imperial rule, a large imperial army leaves Kyoto for Edo to subdue the pro-Tokugawa forces that have gathered there. Hanzō is officially informed that the army will come by way of the Kiso Road and that it will stop at Magome. To his joy, he is also commanded to inform the local inhabitants that the generalissimo will be pleased to take note of whatever complaints they may have against past injustices. He quickly finds, however, that the peasants look upon the coming of the imperial army with apathy; and when at last it arrives, there is hardly a soul in Magome with whom he can share his happiness.

A dozen or so members of the Hirata school, including his friends Keizō and Kōzō, came with the army. They had joined the expedition as cultural advisers. Hanzō wished that the peasants could have seen their happy faces. When he had first heard the news that an army commanded by the young Lord Iwakura was to be sent from Kyoto to Edo he had thought: "If they would only come through Magome—how happy the peasants would be then. Would they not rush to the soldiers and comfort them with offerings of mountain sake and home-made delicacies?" His hope had been realized. Lord Iwakura was now here with the army. Was this not the day the peasants had looked forward to all these years? Surely, they had borne patiently the indescribable hardships of their life under the samurai only in the hope that such a day as this might finally come? . . . They had been told to present their complaints to the *honjin* without fear. But not one peasant had appeared to plead for himself or for others of his class.[125]

It is one of the ironies of Hanzō's life that despite the deep concern he feels for the welfare of the peasants, he never does win their confidence or their affection. He remains throughout his life a strange figure in their eyes. It is not so much the fact of his belonging to a different class, as his bookishness, his seeming impracticality, that separates him from them. They know that he means well, but they suspect his idealism. He ought to spend more time being a *shōya*, they feel, and stop concerning himself so much with abstractions. As far as they are concerned, it makes little difference who rules Japan. After all, were not the imperial soldiers, when they came through Magome, just as demanding, just as arrogant as the *bakufu* men before the Restoration?

125. *Zenshū*, 8: 113.

Of course they are unfair to Hanzō; but it is true also that he does not entirely understand them. Indeed, for all his interest in the peasants of Magome, he is so little aware of their capacity for bitterness and anger that when they take part in a large local uprising, he is quite bewildered. The uprising, involving some one thousand peasants from various villages in the area, takes place in 1868, while Hanzō is away in Kyoto visiting friends. By the time he returns, it is all over. Local acquaintances of his own class try to explain to him why there has been an uprising. The reasons are simple: prices have risen considerably, whereas there has been no increase in the income of the peasants; also, because of the recent conscription into the imperial army of peasant foot-soldiers for the campaign against the Sendai and Aizu clans in the north, many of the villages have found themselves terribly shorthanded. Obvious as these reasons are, however, they do not completely satisfy Hanzō. He simply cannot understand why the peasants did not show more faith in the new government. Anxious to hear what the peasants themselves have to say regarding the uprising, he calls two of the men attached to the Aoyama land to his house, and questions them. These two—they are named Kenkichi and Sōsaku—have known Hanzō all their lives, and are particularly close to him. Yet even they are extremely reticent in his presence.

"Master, I can't tell you," said Kenkichi, rubbing his forehead with his large peasant's hand. "Neither Sōsaku here nor I had anything to do with the affair; but what is done is done, and all of us in the village have agreed not to talk about it."

"I understand perfectly well. I am no more anxious than you are to get any of our men into trouble. What I am concerned about is the future. You are happy, aren't you, that the old days are over? You can't have forgotten how those arrogant samurai used to behave whenever they came here. Why, they used to say quite openly that peasants hadn't the brains to think of anything but what was immediately under their noses. As far as they were concerned, you were no better than tools to be made use of. Your entire life, one might say, consisted in being chased around by samurai who were forever threatening to cut you down. But at last, with the Restoration, things have begun to change. You are happy about it all, aren't you?"

"Of course we are happy."

"I'm glad to hear that."

But Kenkichi's answer seemed to Hanzō rather forced. He felt somehow that Kenkichi was simply trying to please him.[126]

126. *Zenshū*, 8: 171–72.

Hanzō, however, refuses to be discouraged by their reluctance to talk. Finally, Kenkichi, not without irritation at the persistent questioning, says:

"It's not so bad for those who farm for themselves. Their fortune doesn't vary with the times. But what about the likes of us who must work for others? It's these merchant fellows that are the lucky ones these days, I can tell you. It's always the peasant who gets the short end of the stick. At best it's a hand-to-mouth existence for us. We are lucky if we have anything to eat at all. When we run out of the little rice that we do have, we have no choice but to buy some, no matter how expensive it is. And it's no easy matter for us to find cash."

"It's that hard for you, is it? But at a time like this, none of us has an easy time of it. Let me ask you something. It wasn't so long ago that Lord Iwakura passed through. Now, he distributed gifts of money when he stopped here. You should all have got something. What did you do with it?"

"I don't want to seem rude, but how long do you think that kind of money can last? It bought us a drink or two, that's all."

Then suddenly this simple-minded, honest rustic's eyes filled with tears. Sōsaku sat silently beside Kenkichi and continued to look at the floor. He bowed and stood up with his companion. As he was about to walk away from the fireplace, he spoke at last. Sōsaku was a man of few words. "You see, master," he said, "you can't be expected to know what's really going on. Who would tell you?" [127]

Even among the few men in Magome who associate with him more or less on terms of equality, only his neighbor Inosuke has any true sympathy for him. But this Inosuke, though a kind and affectionate friend, lacks Hanzō's intelligence and education and cannot offer the kind of companionship Hanzō sometimes desperately needs. It is, then, at this point in Hanzō's life when he has begun to be aware of his loneliness that his father dies at the age of seventy-one. Theirs has been a strange relationship—trusting and deeply affectionate, yet formal and removed. What has separated them has ultimately been Hanzō's devotion to the royalist cause. Tōson clearly suggests this in the last conversation he reports between the two. Hanzō receives word from the authorities that as part of the reform of the administrative system, Lord Tokugawa of Owari will henceforth be known as prefectural governor of Nagoya. When Hanzō conveys this news to Kichizaemon, the old man cries. Hanzō sits silently, unable to share his father's sadness. [128] Kichizaemon's death is nevertheless a blow to Hanzō. Kichizaemon may not have liked his son's

127. *Zenshū*, 8: 173.
128. *Zenshū*, 8: 229.

modern ideas, but he respected them; he was an intelligent and cultivated man, and he understood Hanzō's love of books and his deep attachment to history. They may have held widely different political opinions; but they were father and son after all and, what was perhaps more important, the only gentlemen in the village. During the wake, Hanzō does something we have never seen him do before. He drinks himself senseless. Perhaps it is out of sorrow purely; or perhaps it is partly from a sense of guilt for not having been able to sympathize fully with his father's conservatism during his last years. Characteristically, Tōson does not tell us.

What makes his isolation in Magome bearable for Hanzō is the thought that soon his faith in the new government will be shown to have been justified. Before long, he is convinced, the new officialdom will put into effect necessary reforms to alleviate the hardship borne for so long by the lowly. Those harsh laws and customs of the Tokugawa era, which were instituted by those that governed to serve their own selfish ends, will be replaced by more charitable ones, designed to help the poor. Thus the closed forests of Kiso, Hanzō is certain, will soon be made accessible to the peasants, who will then be able to take advantage of the one natural resource that is abundant in the area. And during the first year or two of Meiji at least, it begins to seem that perhaps Hanzō's expectation of mercy from the imperial government was not exactly unfounded. Tsuchiya, the new local administrator appointed by the prefectural office at Nagoya, turns out to be honest, sympathetic, and competent. Having been a retainer of the Owari daimyo before the Restoration, he is well acquainted with the condition of the peasants in Kiso. He understands that they must have access to the timber if their lives are to be made easier; and he is ready to persuade his superiors to declare open much of the land that was closed to the public before. Much of his good will is of course due to his having been an Owari samurai; he has always known at least by name the leading rural families of Kiso, and such men as Hanzō and his counterparts from other villages who have appealed to him on behalf of the peasants, he trusts and respects. He is essentially a model feudal official, therefore. The irony of the situation becomes clear when, under the rearrangement of the prefectural system of 1872, Kiso leaves Nagoya Prefecture and becomes a part of Chikuma Prefecture. Tsuchiya before he has had time to solve the problem of the forest lands, has to vacate his post and is replaced by an administrator of the new school. The latter is a modern civil servant who has no traditional ties either with Kiso or the local families. He is interested merely in proving his efficiency to his superiors at the prefectural office in Matsumoto. Under his administration, even those mountains that the Owari daimyo had traditionally left open to the peasants are declared government property and closed. The injustice of this renovation appals Hanzō and the other village headmen of the area. The most active of these, of whom Hanzō is one, decide that they must appeal to the prefectural head office in Matsumoto. They will prepare a petition in which is included a detailed history of the customs pertaining to the forest lands of Kiso and get as many headmen and other important men of the area as possible to sign it. Before it is ready, however, the subprefectural office at Kiso Fukushima, where the local administrator resides, gets wind of their activity. Somewhat unjustly, it is assumed that Hanzō is the ringleader. He is summoned immediately to appear before the officials at Fukushima; there, he is formally notified of his dismissal from the office of village headman.

He hurriedly got himself ready for the return journey. There were people he knew in Fukushima, but he did not want to see them. It had just begun to rain outside. Soon, he was walking in one of those heavy May showers which beat down on the last of the spring flowers and on the fresh green leaves. He was soaked through, but he did not care. Through the wind and the rain he walked on at a steady pace to Uematsu, then to Nojiri. That night, at the inn in Nojiri, he slept badly.

The next morning the sun was out. At last, as he walked under the brilliantly blue sky, he began to feel a little calmer. He thought of his own hopes and disappointments of recent years, and he asked himself: "Was the Restoration intended to be like this?"

Once he stopped by a large stone on the side of the road and placing his straw hat on it, sat down to rest. Beside him was a buckthorn, with its delicate branches and lightly colored leaves. He could see the waters of the Kiso River glittering in the distance. He sat for a while, and pondered.[129]

Tōson's handling of the entire incident is markedly restrained. Hanzō is shown displaying so little emotion over his own misfortune that one is apt to feel either that he is not too deeply affected by his dismissal from office or that Tōson is not quite capable of making full dramatic use of the incident. But actually, the author is purposely understating here. Indeed, the whole of *Before the Dawn* is understated. This is perhaps why so many readers find it dull. So much of what Tōson might have said is left unsaid, so much is barely implied, that Tōson does sometimes, it is true, seem to be demanding more of the reader than he has a right to. But there is no mistaking the suggestion of emotional power, which, because of its very containment, seems all the more moving. Moreover, Tōson is trying to convey to the reader Hanzō's own enormous restraint. Hanzō is a deeply emotional man who cannot show, even to those who are close to him, what he really feels. This inability, or refusal, to give release to his innermost feelings increases his loneliness and becomes, as his suffering grows, an intolerable strain. Later, he does suddenly allow all the bitterness that he has been secretly harboring for so long to come to the surface; but by then he has become an eccentric who is soon to become a drunk and, in the end, a madman.

When he returns to Magome from Fukushima, he says little about his dismissal to others. Even Otami, his wife, can only guess at what her husband must feel. With great subtlety, Tōson suggests both Hanzō's loneliness and his uncommunicativeness in a seemingly insignificant, incidental scene. Hanzō's daughter is about to get married. The wedding will cost money; and though the Aoyama are by no means poor, they, like all such families after the Restoration, are not as securely placed as they were. Moreover, the family is likely to decline further after the loss of their hereditary position. One day, Otami, in order to check the special utensils necessary for the entertainment of wedding guests, goes to the family storehouse. The door to the building is unlocked, and she hears movement upstairs. She goes up and looks in.

She found Hanzō sitting in the room, deep in thought. He had brought out the ancient sword that had been in the Aoyama family for generations, the old hanging scrolls, and the valuable tea utensils that his father had collected during his lifetime. The floor was of wood and unmatted. This was where they kept the chest that Oman, Hanzō's stepmother, had brought with her years ago at the time of her marriage and the chest that Otami herself had brought from Tsumago. These were in the center of the room. Piled up against the walls were the Chinese and Japanese books that Hanzō had collected from the time of his youth. Otami remembered the rumors she had recently been hearing about all the old families in the area who were being forced to sell their valuable possessions. She was suddenly filled with pity for her husband, whom she had never seen looking so pathetic. "He has come here," she thought, "to hide his worry from us."[130]

It is now 1873, and Hanzō is forty-three. All that the authorities have left for him to do is to oversee the education of the children in the village. He has heard too that his friends of the Hirata school, who were so active immediately before and after the Restoration, are now being ignored by the men in power. The retired head of the school, Hirata Tetsutane, is an old man of seventy-two; and his young successor, Nobutane, has just died. "Hanzō felt," Tōson writes, "as though a chill wind had begun to blow."[131] He decides that he must leave Magome to escape from his own sense of failure and uselessness. Perhaps in Tokyo, the authorities will find him something useful to do. In the forlorn hope, then, that his life might not seem so meaningless in new surroundings, he leaves his family behind and goes up to the capital. He has been there before in the days when it was still known as Edo. He finds it much changed.

He wondered whether it was just like this when, in that distant past, Japan first began to import things Chinese. Everything that came from abroad was now assumed to be a symbol of enlightenment. Knock on any head with the top knot cut off, a popular song went, and you'll hear an "enlightened" sound. Those palanquin bearers who used to run about clad only in G-strings, summer and winter, had gone out of fashion. Even the fish vendors with their naked thighs and the Tsukuda clam vendors whose custom it had always been to go scantily clad, now seemed ashamed of themselves in the presence of foreigners. . . .

The strain of living in Tokyo began to tell on him. He felt himself becoming unduly sensitive to everything he saw and heard. In place of the palanquins, rickshaws with single or double seats, and horse-drawn carriages were beginning to appear on the streets. Quite a few people, he noticed, were dressed, but most haphazardly and tentatively, in European clothes. He saw one man wearing a Japanese topcoat over his European suit. Another was dressed completely in European clothes except for his wooden clogs. This man, besides, had recently cut off his top knot, and his hair fell loosely over his shoulders. . . . Yet another was dressed in a kimono, complete with a dashing white sash around his waist, but his feet, alas, were in leather shoes. . . .

He asked himself: "Is this what the Restoration amounts to?" What he saw unfolding before him was not the restoration of the ancient past, but the beginning of a strange new age.[132]

130. *Zenshū*, 8: 295.
131. *Zenshū*, 8: 329.
132. *Zenshū*, 8: 348, 349, 351.

Through the intercession of friends, he is given a not very distinguished post as clerk in the Ministry of Religious Affairs, which was once controlled by members of the Hirata school. It is not what it used to be. The purity and zeal of the early days of the Restoration have disappeared, and the ministry is now peopled with questionably educated and vulgar civil servants. One day, much to his shock, he overhears his colleagues laughing over a lewd joke; he discovers that the subject of the joke is none other than the great Motoori Norinaga, whom he has revered all his life. The work he has to do at the office gives him no solace either. Every day, he must look through letters of inquiry that come to the ministry from priests of various faiths in the provinces. Those that come to him, at any rate, are dishearteningly banal. In a typical letter, a Buddhist priest asks if he might, when not conducting a religious service, wear clothes befitting a citizen of a civilized country—meaning, of course, European clothes. In another, a priest asks if his family might engage in commerce and use the temple as premises.[133] It is not long before Hanzō feels compelled to resign his post. He must keep whatever self-respect he still has.

His acquaintances tell him that the rectorship of a small Shinto shrine in remote Hida is open. If he so wishes, they will recommend him for the post. Hanzō really does not want to be exiled; but he has no choice, and he accepts. It is while he is awaiting confirmation of his new appointment that he does something which the people of Magome, who hear of it, come to regard later as having been the first sign of an approaching madness. The occasion is the public procession of the emperor and his court through the streets of Tokyo.

He had a new folding fan with him as he left his rooms. On it was written a poem he had recently composed. He did not then intend to show the poem to others. He had written it, rather, for his own edification. It had grown out of the proud thought that though born a humble countryman, he was as concerned as anyone for the future of his country. It expressed his conviction that he and every other Japanese owed it to their children to stop this tide of Europeanization that was sweeping the country. This was his poem: "The crab's hole, if forgotten, will one day cause the dike to crumble." With the fan in hand he stood in the crowd, waiting for the procession.

Half an hour passed. Then he heard the stirring sound of galloping horses coming towards them. It was the advance guard of the household cavalry.

133. *Zenshū*, 8: 361.
11*

Hanzō could feel the general thrill of anticipation around him as these horsemen galloped past with their ensigns held high. It was at this point that he was
overcome by a sudden, uncontrollable desire to present to the emperor his
fan as a token of his devotion. Thinking that the first coach that approached
them carried attendants and not the emperor, he hurriedly pushed his way
through to the forefront of the crowd. He was now acting on pure impulse.
He threw the fan into the coach, then drew back a step or two, and knelt
down. He bowed low until his head touched the ground. Thus he remained.

There was confusion all around him. "A petitioner, that's what he is,"
someone was saying. Other voices, more angry, were being hurled in his
direction. A policeman rushed up to him and grabbed his arm. The crowd
began to move towards him threateningly.[134]

He learns too late that he has actually thrown the fan into the
emperor's coach. He is immediately taken to jail where he is kept
for a few days until the magistrates are ready to pass sentence.
His background is eminently respectable, however, and he has
intended no harm. He is admonished, made to pay a fine, and
confined to his lodgings for a period of fifty days. The sentence is
therefore a nominal one. Even his prospective appointment to the
rectorship is not questioned. But the experience hurts Hanzō
deeply.

He spends four years in the country shrine. When at last he
returns to Magome, he is a changed person. He is more withdrawn than ever; also, he has become prone to sudden emotional
outbursts. What makes his return particularly bitter is the death
shortly before of Inosuke, his only friend in Magome. On the
hundredth day after Inosuke's death, a memorial service is held.
Hanzō is one of those present. He has since his return said little
of his friend's death. And through the early part of the service he
remains outwardly calm. But as the priest begins to recite the final
prayer, he suddenly breaks down. "Oblivious of the presence of
others," Tōson writes, "he wept unashamedly."[135]

It is now 1880. The village elders receive the happy news that
that summer the emperor will make a tour of the Kiso Road and
that he and his retinue will stop for a brief rest at Magome. The
villagers begin at once to prepare for the great occasion. Hanzō,
however, is not asked to participate. By birth and education, he is
unquestionably the most distinguished man in the village. He
ought of course to be on the reception committee. But the

134. *Zenshū*, 8: 376–77.
135. *Zenshū*, 8: 440.

cautious and unimaginative elders have heard of Hanzō's eccentric behavior in Tokyo, and they are afraid that he may once more
misbehave himself. They ask his family to make sure that on the
day of the emperor's visit he is kept well in the background.
These men cannot be expected to understand what the emperor
has meant, and still means, to a man of Hanzō's convictions. Had
the Restoration not taken place and had it been the shogun that
was about to pay Magome a visit, they would have been just as
excited and just as impressed. And so perhaps they do not intend
to be quite as cruel to Hanzō as they in fact are. After all, as
Tōson reminds us with perhaps a touch of bitterness, of those in
the village that could read and write, there was hardly one that
did not owe his literacy to Hanzō's devoted tutelage.[136]

There is little hope left in Hanzō's existence. He tries to find
some consolation in teaching the young, but that is hardly enough.
In order perhaps to forget his disillusionment and loneliness, he
begins to drink heavily. Soon, he is a confirmed drunkard. One
day, Katsushige, who studied under him in the days before the
Restoration, pays him a visit. He has come from Ochiai, a village
miles away from Magome, to console his former teacher. He has
a gift, a flask of sake.

When Hanzō saw what Katsushige had brought, he opened his eyes wide and
with the unabashed happiness of a young child said: "Well, well, Katsushige,
so you've brought me some sake." There was not a soul in his family now who
did not remind him daily that a man in retirement ought to lead a life of
moderation. The only person Hanzō knew these days who would have the
kindness to bring him sake to comfort his lonely existence was Katsushige, his
faithful disciple.

"Katsushige, I know I shouldn't say this, but it seems that all my family
want to do is to make me grow old."

"But master, they are only thinking of your welfare."

"As I sit here from morning to night with nothing to do but stare at the
mountains, memories of the last half of my life keep coming back to taunt me. I
can't live like this, doing nothing, forever."

Hanzō got up and picking up the flask as though it were the most precious
thing in the world, walked away towards the kitchen to put it away. In a
minute or two he came back, grinning happily.[137]

By the year 1884, the Aoyama house has declined considerably.
Sōta, Hanzō's eldest son and the head of the family ever since

136. *Zenshū*, 8: 452.
137. *Zenshū*, 8: 464–65.

Hanzō's return from his exile in Hida, informs his father one day that they have incurred, over the course of some ten years, debts totalling three thousand six hundred yen (a large sum for those days, especially in rural Japan). They will have to sell some of their land in order to pay these debts. The news comes as a shock to Hanzō, who has never been very realistic about money. But what really hurts him is the realization that not only his neighbors, but his own family, believe that the debts were incurred largely because of his mismanagement and irresponsibility. And when he learns that the family council has decided to impose a set of restrictions on his future conduct, he feels totally helpless and defeated. He must, he is told, refrain from interfering with family affairs, which are properly the concern of Sōta; he must not drink more than a fraction of a pint of sake a day; and for pocket money he will be given one yen a month. He has no choice but to acquiesce. After he has formally agreed to abide by the rules, he turns to his wife and says bitterly: "What a way to grow old."[138]

Soon after, in his fifty-sixth year, Hanzō clearly begins to lose his sanity. "Strange things began to happen inside his mind," Tōson writes. "At times, when he was unusually depressed, the arabesque figures on the sliding doors of his room would seem to move. And sometimes, the teacups and pots around him would seem to have taken on sexual characteristics and transformed themselves into manifestations of Yin and Yang."[139] He imagines too that he is being followed by shapes, shadowy yet monstrous. "A weird creature was hiding in the corner of our garden," he tells his wife on one occasion. "A frightening fellow he was. There he crouched, waiting to get at me. I couldn't stand it, so I set fire to a bundle of old leaves and threw it at him. There's no need for you to worry, though. He's gone now."[140]

He is regarded, however, more as an eccentric than as a madman by the villagers until one day he sets fire to the village temple. The Zen temple was founded by the first Aoyama to settle in Magome, and his descendants have always been its leading patrons. The temple graveyard is where all of Hanzō's ancestors are buried. And the incumbent rector, an intelligent and decent man, has never shown any animosity to Hanzō despite the

138. *Zenshū*, 8: 477.
139. *Zenshū*, 8: 493.
140. *Zenshū*, 8: 494.

latter's avowed hatred of Buddhism. Thus what Hanzō does is a terrible thing. Fortunately, the fire is stopped before it has done much damage. Now, the villagers are thoroughly frightened of Hanzō. They insist that the family lock him up and make sure he is never again permitted to wander about in Magome. There is a wood-shed at the back of the Aoyama house. The family call in carpenters and have them convert it into a little prison. When it is ready for habitation, Sōta, accompanied by other men, approaches his father. He has a rope in his hand. He says:

"Father, I have no right to be doing such a thing, but you are ill. Please forgive me."

Hanzō looked at the people around him. He knew them well: they were all either close relations or villagers he had taught and in whom he had put so much hope. He felt a sudden pain. "So all of you think I'm mad," he said, and began to cry quietly. And when his son came up to him apologetically with the rope, he put his arms behind him willingly and allowed himself to be tied.

Dusk had fallen on this late September day. Through the growing darkness Hanzō was led from his rooms to the woodshed. His manservant Sakichi [who had worked for him ever since they were both young] was waiting under the persimmon tree by the storehouse. He knelt and bowed his head as his master, so different from the man he used to know, walked past. Thus he remained in this dark spot for a long time.[141]

Hanzō lasts no more than two months in his cell. Perhaps he has lost the will to live. Tōson does not say. Shortly before his death, Katsushige once more comes all the way from Ochiai to see him.

Making sure that there was no one else about, Katsushige approached the crudely fashioned bars. He heard his teacher's voice saying, "Here comes the enemy." The very tone of the voice, thought Katsushige, belonged to someone who had lost all contact with the rest of the world. Anxiously he said: "Master, it is I, Katsushige."

The unexpected visit of Katsushige seemed to bring Hanzō back to reality. He came to the window. His appearance shocked Katsushige. His hair had obviously not been combed for days, and under the dirt and the beard, his face was deathly pale. He had not yet lost all of his awareness, however. After a long silence, he said: "Katsushige, I have finally come to this. I shall die without ever seeing the sun again." He gripped the bars and gazed at his beloved pupil.

"Please don't talk like that," said Katsushige. "As soon as you get better, you'll be able to go back to the house. And when that time comes, I shall be here to take you out of this place. All of us are eagerly waiting for that happy day. Incidentally, this is the season when people in the old days used to drink to celebrate the chrysanthemums—remember? And so I thought I'd bring along a flask of your favorite Ochiai sake. It must be some time since you last had any."

Katsushige brought out a flask and a small wooden cup. Hanzō stood still and listened attentively to the sound of the sake coming out of the narrow spout. He was almost beside himself with pleasurable anticipation. Eagerly he took the cup which Katsushige held out to him through the bars and drank the sake down as though it were nectar of paradise, the like of which he had never tasted before. Katsushige refilled the cup, and Hanzō drank again.

Next to Hanzō's cell was a little room used by his relatives who took turns nursing him. Katsushige thought he heard someone moving about there and decided to leave Hanzō for a while. What these two wanted to say to each other could be said only when they were alone. Katsushige retired to the little room and waited. He was about to get up to go and see Hanzō again when he heard his teacher talking to himself in the cell. The voice was saying: "What's become of Katsushige? Isn't he here any more? Of course he isn't. He's left me here in this hole and gone back to Ochiai. He really doesn't care. He can't fool me with his smooth talk. Who knows, he too may be one of those monsters."

Katsushige could not bear to hear any more. He went outside and hiding in the bamboo thicket at the back, began to weep violently.[142]

In the last act of Hanzō's life that Tōson describes, he is shown to have gone totally mad. Three villagers, wishing to see how Hanzō is, are walking towards the woodshed. Suddenly, Hanzō begins to throw his own excrement through the bars at the approaching visitors. He imagines that he is some medieval general fighting a battle and that the three men are the enemy about to attack. Immediately after describing this pathetic little incident, Tōson announces with an abruptness that is characteristic of his later style, the death of Hanzō.

All was ended. It was a few days later, when the month of November was drawing to a close, that he lay down to die in the wretched woodshed. . . . Once, shortly before he drew his last breath, he opened his eyes wide. But by then he could see nothing; nor could he hear his wife Otami's voice as she called to him. He died at sunrise. He was aged fifty-six.[143]

This long and dark novel comes to an end as Hanzō's relatives and acquaintances go to the temple graveyard on the day before the funeral to inspect the spot where he is to be buried. Sakichi, Kenkichi, and Sōsaku, the three peasants who were perhaps fondest of Hanzō, are already there, digging the grave. The group

142. *Zenshū*, 8: 530–31.
143. *Zenshū*, 8: 534.

stand there for a while, talking of Hanzō; then one by one they begin to leave the scene. Finally only Katsushige and the three peasants are left.

Katsushige remembered in sorrow those last few words his teacher had spoken to him: "I shall die without ever seeing the sun again."

He heard one of the men saying, "We'll soon be finished." Then there were grunts as they started to dig again. The grave had to be large, for Hanzō was to be buried lengthwise according to Shinto custom. The mound at the side of the grave grew higher as the men continued to dig. The strong smell of newly turned earth filled the air. The sound of the hoes, as they hit the ground one after the other, cut through the surrounding stillness. Katsushige stood and listened in pain.[144]

Tōson died in 1943, at the age of seventy-two, while writing the third chapter of his next novel, *The Eastern Gate* (*Tōhō no mon*).

144. *Zenshū*, 8: 542–43.

Bibliography

Japanese works cited in this book

Sōseki

Sōseki zenshū kankōkai, ed. *Sōseki zenshū*. 20 vols. Tokyo, 1928.
Akamon bungakukai, ed. *Natsume Sōseki*. Tokyo, 1944.
Ara Masato. *Hyōden Natsume Sōseki*. Tokyo, 1960.
Etō Jun. *Natsume Sōseki*. Tokyo, 1960.
Iwagami Jun'ichi. *Sōseki nyūmon*. Tokyo, 1959.
Komiya Toyotaka. *Shirarezaru Sōseki*. Tokyo, 1951.
———. *Natsume Sōseki*. 3 vols. Tokyo, 1953.
Natsume Kyōko. *Sōseki no omoide*. Tokyo, 1929.
Senuma Shigeki. *Natsume Sōseki*. Tokyo, 1962.

Tōson

Shimazaki Tōson zenshū. 19 vols. Tokyo, 1948–52.
Hirano Ken. *Gendai sakka-ron zenshū, 2: Shimazaki Tōson*. Tokyo, 1957.
Itō Shinkichi. *Shimazaki Tōson*. Tokyo, 1947.
Kamei Katsuichirō. *Shimazaki Tōson-ron*. Tokyo, 1954.
Maruyama Shizuka. *Gendai bungaku kenkyū*. Tokyo, 1956.
Masamune Hakuchō. "Shimazaki Tōson," *Gendai Nihon bungaku zenshū, 8: Shimazaki Tōson-shū*. Tokyo, 1953.
Satō Haruo and Uno Kōji, ed. *Meiji bungaku sakka-ron*. 2 vols. Tokyo, 1943.
Senuma Shigeki. *Hyōden Shimazaki Tōson*. Tokyo, 1959.

A selected list of works on modern Japanese literature that may be of interest to the nonspecialist reader

Etō, Jun. "An Undercurrent in Modern Japanese Literature." *Journal of Asian Studies* 18 (May, 1964): 433–45.
———. "Natsume Sōseki: a Japanese Meiji Intellectual." *American Scholar* 34 (1965): 603–19.
Hibbett, Howard S. "The Portrait of the Artist in Japanese Fiction." *Far Eastern Quarterly* 14 (1955): 347–54.
———. "Tradition and Trauma in the Contemporary Japanese Novel." *Daedalus*, Fall, 1966: 925–40.
Keene, Donald. *Japanese Literature: An Introduction for Western Readers*. New York, 1958.

Keene, Donald, comp. and ed. *Modern Japanese Literature: An Anthology.* New York, 1956.

McClellan, Edwin. "The Impressionistic Tendency in Some Modern Japanese Writers," *Chicago Review* 17 (1965): 48–60.

Morris, Ivan, ed. *Modern Japanese Stories: An Anthology.* Rutland, Vermont, and Tokyo, 1962.

Ryan, Marleigh. *Japan's First Modern Novel: Ukigumo of Futabatei Shimei.* New York, 1967.

Seidensticker, Edward. *Kafū the Scribbler: The Life and Writings of Nagai Kafū, 1879–1959.* Stanford, 1965.

———. "The Unshapen Ones," *The Japan Quarterly,* 11 (1964): 64–69.

Articles of more specialized interest

Mathy, Francis. "Kitamura Tōkoku: The Early Years." *Monumenta Nipponica,* 18 (1963): 1–44.

———. "Kitamura Tōkoku: Essays on the Inner Life." *Monumenta Nipponica* 19 (1964): 66–110.

———. "Kitamura Tōkoku: Final Essays." *Monumenta Nipponica* 20 (1965): 41–63.

Roggendorf, Joseph. "Shimazaki Tōson, a Maker of the Modern Japanese Novel." *Monumenta Nipponica* 7 (1951): 40–66.

Viglielmo, Valdo H. "An Introduction to the Later Novels of Natsume Sōseki." *Monumenta Nipponica* 19 (1964): 1–36.

A selected list of translations of Sōseki's novels. (Unfortunately, there are no translations of Tōson's novels.)

Kokoro: Le Pauvre Coeur des Hommes. Tr. by Horiguchi Daigaku and Georges Bonneau. Paris, 1939.

Kokoro. Tr. by Edwin McClellan. Chicago, 1957. (Paperback edition, 1967.)

The Three-Cornered World (Kusamakura). Tr. by Alan Turney. London, 1965.

For a fuller bibliography, see *Japanese Literature in European Languages,* compiled by the Japan P.E.N. Club, Tokyo, 1961. (Supplement: Tokyo, 1964)

Index